# EPIPHANY
## THE DESIGNATED BULLET

### MARSHON PEOPLES

MARSHON PEOPLES

EPIPHANY

Copyright © 2022 by MarShon Peoples.

All rights reserved. No part of this publication may be reproduced, distributed, or transmitted in any form or by any means, including photocopying, recording, or other electronic or mechanical methods, without the prior written permission of the publisher, except in the case of brief quotations embodied in critical reviews and certain other noncommercial uses permitted by copyright law. For permission requests, write to the publisher, addressed "Attention: Permissions Coordinator," at the address below.

This publication has been made available and printed by YAH-Scribe Publishing, LLC in the United States of America

Editor: Aleah M'Poko
Promoter: Keith Farmer

**ISBN Information**
ISBN: 979-8-3507-2521-6

**Version: February 7, 2024**

**Author Information**
peoplesunlimintedllc@gmail.com
www.goodepeoples.com

**Publisher Information**
www.yahscribe.com

# Foreword

## by Tera Carissa Hodges

If you have ever recognized a painful yet unexplainable pattern in your life that just didn't make sense, yet it shows up, almost rhythmically in different stages of your life, *Epiphany: The Designated Bullet* is for you as it affirms, you are not alone.

As a licensed minister, life coach, empowerment speaker, and author, I can tell you after two decades of ministering to thousands, people live decades experiencing patterns, that through one lens can be seen as a foreshadowing of a life-changing event that will either launch them or level them. Yet through another lens, this can be interpreted as the enemy trying to put forth *his* will for their life, which requires deep prayer to resist it, bind it, and thwart it.

The consistent yet nuanced premature appointments MarShon had with death throughout his life is no different. It both alarms the reader, yet prepares the reader. It was almost as if God was giving MarShon "hints" and glimpses as to what was destined to happen in his life. Yet, one can't help but wonder, were previous life events God foreshadowing with hints or God warning and giving prophetic insight on what to pray against?

It's the age-old question we all ask ourselves when faced with what our society would deem unfavorable circumstances in our lives: "Did this *have* to happen?" "Was this *supposed* to happen?" or, "Did I not heed the signs, warnings, gut feelings and red flags?"

As a woman of faith who believes and teaches "the chosen" are sent here by God on assignment to live a purposeful—not perfect or pain-free, but purposeful—life for *a* greater good and *the* greater good, and that *all* things work together for our good... including our mistakes, disobedience, short-comings, and blind spots,

MarShon's testimony throughout *Epiphany* affirms just that. Whether destined by God or determined through free will choice, if our faith in God remains intact, it all works together for our good.

Similar to how scripture tells us Jesus was sent to earth to endure pain and suffering for a purpose greater than Himself (John 3:16), one can only assume God had it in mind to create MarShon's life for the sole purpose of using it to testify for the benefit of others how God is a keeper, healer, deliverer, redeemer, restorer and much more.

Undoubtedly, God has used MarShon's life to testify to who God is, at a cost that I am not sure many of us could have paid. And yet through MarShon's faith in God—-like Job, he endured and continues to endure. Subsequently, *Epiphany* takes the reader on a journey that makes you wonder how could such a seemingly normal life experience such extraordinary circumstances if not purposed by God?

How could a person seemingly so committed to living right, experience so much wrong if he were not under "attack" by the enemy fighting to have *his* will for MarShon's life prevail? How could a person seemingly so gifted experience brushes with success *and* failure if being an example for others was not a part of his destiny?

These are not just questions a reader will ask of MarShon's life, but their own, as I am a firm believer, life happens to us all. If you are looking for an example of how to live, how to have faith, how to hold on, evolve and reinvent after a series of storms, *Epiphany* is an excellent companion.

Join me in being inspired by one man's journey to become enlightened despite the darkness that could have overcome him.

# Editor's Note

## by Aleah M'Poko

*Epiphany* was introduced to me as a job. At the time, I couldn't have imagined that it would impact me as profoundly as it has. When I received the initial draft, I was vaguely familiar with Mr. Peoples' testimony—in short, surviving a gunshot to the head.

I had no idea what to expect from the book other than a thoroughly elaborated account of this story. I would soon discover, however, that even before having a bullet lodged in his skull and living to tell the story, Mr. Peoples was no stranger to miracles and mighty moves of God. *Epiphany* walks us through a series of remarkable illustrations of God's goodness, mercy, and grace.

Not only are we told, in this book, of the countless ways in which God delivered him from the grasp of adversity, but we get a front-row seat to some of the key experiences—both joys and hardships—that shaped a man whose lifelong walk with God has changed the course of countless lives for the Kingdom.

I was taken aback by how immersed I became in Mr. Peoples' lived experience as I worked my way through the pages of the draft. I was moved by each account of the people who have greatly impacted his life and how he so generously honors them. I found myself in tears as he described acts of sacrifice, boldness, and discernment when it would have been much easier to give in to despair. In addition, his openness and transparency make him highly relatable and remind me of how faithful God is to meet us where we're at.

Mr. Peoples' humble, authentic, and enthusiastic approach to story-telling makes *Epiphany* both readable and captivating. This book is alive with a unique balance of humor and vulnerability. It's an effortless reflection of Mr. Peoples' reverence for God and his heart for people. His exceptional narrative memory—evident in the consistency between his writing and verbal accounts in conversation—makes for a rich reading experience, bringing the book to life and inviting you into every moment he describes.

*Epiphany* is more than just a book; it's an experience—an opportunity to witness the character of God and reflect on the role He's played in your own life—and an appeal to seek a personal, intimate relationship with your Father so your life, too, can reflect His goodness, mercy, and grace.

# Prelude

## by Keith "Big Poppa" Toney

I am honored to be a part of this great opportunity. We came to Messias Temple in the early eighties. That's when I met Shon and his lovely mother. We have four children all around the same age.

I remember you coming to our home and visiting many times; you and Kevin my son were very good friends. You and my kids were a part of the Youth Choir. I remember you having such a great love for the Lord, growing up and being a great example to the other young people.

We loved when you came to our home, you would bring so much joy with you. You were very close to your mother (she was a great Baker). It was just the two of you, and you were very close. After you became a young man you still had a love for the youth. My son Kevin called us and said you got shot in the head because as a Youth Leader, you were trying to make sure the young people were safe while at an event. We were in disbelief and started praying immediately for your full recovery. I prayed, "Oh God don't let him die!" I had to rebuke the enemy because of the thoughts he was bringing to my mind about death.

The Word of the Lord says the prayers of the righteous avail much. When I tell you the saints were praying; they touched the throne of God, praying to spare your life and to make a full recovery. I know you're saying, "You can't make me doubt Him; I know too much about Him."

I thank God for you, young man. I thank God for touching your body and restoring it to full health. Who wouldn't serve a God like this? Thank you so much and may God continue to bless you.

# Contents

Bullet 1..................................................................1

Bullet 2..................................................................5

Bullet 3..................................................................11

Bullet 4..................................................................17

Bullet 5..................................................................22

Bullet 6..................................................................28

Bullet 7..................................................................35

Bullet 8..................................................................42

Bullet 9..................................................................47

Bullet 10................................................................55

Bullet 11................................................................60

Bullet 12................................................................76

Bullet 13................................................................84

Bullet 14................................................................94

Bullet 15................................................................102

Bullet 16................................................................118

Bullet 17..............................................................125

Bullet 18..............................................................133

Bullet 19..............................................................139

Bullet 20..............................................................152

Bullet 21..............................................................159

Bullet 22..............................................................164

Bullet 23..............................................................172

Bullet 24..............................................................177

Bullet 25..............................................................180

Bullet 26..............................................................186

Bullet 27..............................................................190

Bullet 28..............................................................199

Bullet 29..............................................................207

Bullet 30..............................................................218

Bullet 31..............................................................230

Bullet 32..............................................................234

Bullet 33..............................................................243

# BULLET ONE

I am MarShon Peoples. I was born August 21, 1974, at Blodgett Memorial Hospital in Grand Rapids, Michigan. I am the only child of my mother, Doris Ann Peoples. The surname "Peoples" has French origins, deriving from the lineage of King Papys le Bref of the Carolingian Dynasty. My great-grandfather, Otis Peoples, grandfather Monroe Peoples and grandmother Cherries Peoples are all from Starkville, Mississippi, Native Land of the Choctaw people and home of "Mother Mound." Big Momma Plummie and Big Momma Stacy Williams—Grandma Cherrie's Mom—were Choctaw Natives.

Right across the Mississippi River is New Orleans, where one of the main entry ports into the U.S. is and where descendants of the Carlovingian Dynasty had French and Hebrew sharecroppers. These people were not quite slaves but definitely servants to the Carlovingian Nobles. This historical DNA melting pot makes my family bloodline part Creole.

# EPIPHANY

I was raised in Ypsilanti, Michigan, a small town located 30 miles from Detroit, also known as "Motown"—the city that gave us such musical legends as The Spinners, Stevie Wonder, and Aretha Franklin, to name a few.

The term "the real McCoy"—another way of saying "the real thing"—was coined in Ypsilanti when several competitors of Black French-Canadian engineer Elijah McCoy tried and failed to make counterfeit replicas of the lubrication system McCoy invented for steam engines. The term was used to make reference to his invention as an authentic product. Ironically though, Amtrak doesn't stop in our historical Depot Town in Ypsilanti.

Today, Ypsilanti is home to some great restaurants and wonderful sights. The delicious Swanson Burger, sold at Biggie's (founded and owned by Victor Swanson: www.biggiestasteofsoul.com) came out of Ypsilanti. The town was even mentioned in the May 2019 issue of Forbes Magazine.

Elijah McCoy (1844-1929)
Inventor of lubrication systems for steam engines

**Read Forbes article in the May 2019 issue:**
https://www.forbes.com/sites/lavanyasunkara/2019/05/30/six-reasons-to-visit-ann-arbors-sister-city-of-ypsilanti/amp/).

EPIPHANY

# BULLET TWO

I know it sounds very cliché to say that all my life, I would often look in the mirror wondering, "Why am I here?" I often looked at my hands, feeling as if I was inside of something looking outward. My name alone—MarShon Peoples—came with its own challenges. When I was a child, kids were innocently cruel, calling me "Martian People," "Alien Nation," "Mars Bar," "Space Man," "Enemy Mine," and my favorite, "Marvin the Martian." As I got older, I simply embraced those cruel names by laughing and saying, "You're just saying I'm out of this world."

I can remember when I was very young—as early as 3 years old—mostly being around adults. Namely, my great grandma, my grandma, my granddad, my aunts and uncles, and my cousins. If I wasn't with them, I would be with my mother and her friends.

I learned a lot by just being around. Back then a child was not to speak unless spoken to. You waited till the adults were done talking, or in emergency cases you kindly, politely excused yourself by saying, "Excuse me, but I have an emergency." And it better be a real emergency too!

EPIPHANY

I observed the love and laughter that seemed to fill each house we entered. We often just "stopped by" to visit loved ones or to bring something to them, something that we are greatly missing and needing in our lives today.

At 3 years old, I started at Lindbergh Elementary in Muskegon Heights, Michigan. My Aunt Renee would walk me to school right around the corner from my grandparents' house. I even remember Ms. Kristy, my preschool teacher.

My Aunt Renee would take me everywhere! I would love going to different spots with her, seeing new things in the city. We'd listen to music all the time! Everyone would blast their music out of these big, long cars nicknamed a Deuce and a Quarter. It took so long to turn the car that you had to turn yesterday for the car to actually turn tomorrow. And they had 8 track tape players in the car! Yep, I know, just 8 tracks… but YouTube it: songs were super long back then, lol.

At the age of 4 (1978), my mother moved us from Muskegon Heights, Michigan, to Ypsilanti, Michigan, where I was raised. As a single mother she did the best she could and made the move she believe to be best for us.

I didn't meet my biological father Gregory Kenneth Goode until I was 29 years old, just 8 years before I met the designated bullet I call Epiphany.

Looking back on my life now, I realize just how powerful those family times were. My best friend at the time (now cousin by marriage) was Sadot—now Dr. Karriem Sadot Watson of Chicago. We played together all the time. Sometimes we even got to be with other kids from our church, like Jason and Aaron Turner.

Sadot and I, along with Sadot's older sisters, my aunts, my cousins, and my mom, were all so very close. They took us to many activities, like concerts, the carnival, bowling, the beach, and, of course, going to eat! I'm talking about restaurants like the delightful Scribb's Pizza and Flamingo's Mexican-home of the Chili, Chips n Cheese, two of the most popular spots in town. We also some of the folks who put the "Soul" in Soul Food. Just ask members of Christ Temple Church in Muskegon Heights, Michigan, where we all attended and where the late great Diocesan Bishop of the PAW, Willie Lee Burrel, presided.

# EPIPHANY

The sense of family was different back then. We would go over to each other's houses, fellowship, laugh and eat together even if that wasn't the reason you came over. The love that was given when anyone showed up was, "Have something to eat; let me make you a plate." I can't help but reminisce on preparing the meals with my grandma in that hot little kitchen (it was a big kitchen when I was little, though!)..

On that note, I have to mention our family barbecue sauce. You could eat it alone with some bread and it makes you wanna bite your whole hand off! My Uncle Bell Totten's sauce (rest in the Lord) is the original, with a slightly sweet flavor, and my Granddad's (some call him Uncle Mun; rest in the Lord) sauce was the same but on the spicy side. People from Messias Temple call it "that Muskegon Sauce." Oh! Just thinking about the delicious aroma, the smells, the seasonings, spices, and conversation makes me remember what togetherness is… Family.

Bishop William Lee Burrel (1927 - 1995)
Pentecostal Assemblies of the World

EPIPHANY

# BULLET THREE

The church we attended most of my life is called Messias Temple Church in Ypsilanti It was originally located on Monroe Street and later relocated to Harriet Street—also on the south side of Ypsilanti. The pastor was an old, regal man of God by the name of Jesse Ross. He and I became very close as his wife Ethel and granddaughter Rebecca, nicknamed "Becky," would often look after me while my mother was at work.

Pastor Ross was a very serious, strict man of the Holy scriptures. He had a fair complexion with these steel gray eyes that would command respect when you looked into them. His hair was a pale white with speckled hints of gray that gave him a wise and majestic look. He would sit me on his lap, read me different Bible stories, and frequently spoke of "The Remission of Sin." He would speak of how Jesus died to pay the price of death and to wash away my sins with His blood that was shed for me.

I remember asking at the tender age of 5, "How can Jesus wash away my sin with blood?" Pastor Ross would read to me, running his crooked old index finger across every word so I could follow along in the pages of Holy Writ. He would say, "Shon... I need you to see God in His Word."

He then turned to the passage of Hebrews 6, verses 1 and 2, taking me into what is called The 6 Principles of the Doctrine of Christ or Messiah.

## 6 Principles of the Doctrine of Christ

1. Repentance From Dead Works
2. Faith toward God
3. Doctrine of Baptisms
4. Laying of Hands
5. Resurrection of The Dead
6. Eternal Judgment

At this young age—5 years old—I thought he was talking about 6 school principles and the kind of doctor you find in a hospital. It's funny when you think of the simplicity of a child's mind.

This passage, found in Hebrews chapter 6, became the main subject of my talks with Pastor Ross, starting every lesson with, "Shon... Always remember nothing to nothing but Jesus." And "Jesus died, but He what?" and I would answer him back, "He got up!" Although I didn't know it at the time, he was answering my question by teaching me about the death, burial, resurrection, and ascension of our Lord Jesus Christ, i.e., The Gospel. This is the foundation that, today, I live by and walk upon toward God.

## Hebrews 6:1-2

> Therefore leaving the principles of the doctrine of Christ, let us go on unto perfection; not laying again the foundation of repentance from dead works, and of faith toward God, of the doctrine of baptisms, and of laying on of hands, and of resurrection of the dead, and of eternal judgment.

Pastor Ross would lead me through the Bible, especially the Old Testament scriptures of Abraham, saying, "See, Shon... God promised Abraham something that He wants to give to you." When I asked, "What did God promise Abraham?" Pastor Ross answered, "The Kingdom of God." I was amazed. "Woooow! A Kingdom?" I questioned, "Well, what about Abraham? I don't want to take Abraham's promise." Even at 5, I'd had people make a promise to me and not keep it. I remember then feeling sad because they'd broken their promise.

# EPIPHANY

I didn't want Abraham to have that same feeling of sadness. Pastor Ross then explained—still using the sixth chapter of Hebrews—that God could not lie. He said God wanted to share that same promise He made unto Abraham with all who believed in Him (Mark 16:15, 16; Galatians 3:18-29; Hebrew 6:1-20).

After this explanation, I decided I wanted this Kingdom and the God who died to shed His blood for me. "Elder Ross?" I asked, "How do I get the Kingdom that God promised?" Pastor Ross answered strong, slow, stern, and deep, "You must be born again to see and enter the Kingdom of God. You must believe, repent, be baptized in Jesus' Name, and be filled with the gift of God's Holy Ghost."

He then read me these scriptures in the same manner as before, leading me with his old, crooked index finger: St. John 3:1-16 and St. John 7:37-39. He concluded with Acts 2:38, 39, and I quote, "Then Peter said unto them, Repent, and be baptized every one of you in the Name of Jesus Christ for the remission of sins, and ye shall receive the gift of the Holy Ghost. For the promise is unto you, and to your children, and to all that are afar off, even as many as the Lord our God shall call."

I was baptized that year at the age of 5 by Pastor Jesse Ross. I remember he cradled me in his arms like a baby and whispered to me, "After I pray to God for you, I want you to hold your nose and mouth closed from when I put you under the water until I bring you back out." I said, "Okay."

He prayed, "Dearly beloved, upon the confession of your faith, concerning the death, burial, and resurrection of our Lord and Savior Jesus Christ and our confidence in the blessed Word of God, I do now indeed baptize you in the Name of our Lord Jesus Christ for the remission of sins and ye shall receive the gift of the Holy Ghost." The water chilled my body but not my soul.

Elder Jesse Ross (April 8, 1908 - June 7, 1991)

EPIPHANY

# BULLET FOUR

I remember attending Perry School for kindergarten. I had Mrs. Rice as a teacher. But I also remember that, since I was only 4 years old when we first got to Ypsilanti, the Ypsilanti school system wouldn't let me start kindergarten, even though I knew all my colors, all my letters, all my numbers, all my shapes, and I could even read a little bit. They still wouldn't let me in because of my age. You might remember I already attended preschool in Muskegon when I was 3. So, my mother had to enroll me in Head Start instead.

I remember a lot of the kids didn't know the difference between the number 3 and the letter 'E', and they were writing their letters backwards. I was helping a lot of them write their ABCs and one, two threes. One teacher told me they had to do the work themselves, and then they put me in this trailer away from the kids that had a two-window mirror—we could still kind of see through it, even as kids.

I didn't know why I was there, but they let us play with different things and read books. That definitely was not the last time I felt singled out in school. I learned there was a huge difference between learning at church and learning in school.

# EPIPHANY

I remember it was then that my mother and I stayed with Jewel Stallworth in a little apartment above Elder Melvin Bass' family's home. They had a boxelder tree in front of the house at that time. The boxelder bugs were everywhere! Jewel didn't mind them, though. She wouldn't let me kill them either. She called the bugs her friends. So they became my friends too!

Elder and Sister Bass were the staple couple most people looked up to at our little Messias Temple Church and throughout the town. They would also have many guest speakers (who would come from out of town for our special services) stay in their guest room and would regularly host the most outstanding Bible studies in their home.

I would sit and listen as the adults exchanged their Biblical knowledge. I would be in a wonderland sort of state as they told story after story of their encounters with the marvelous works of God. Miracle after miracle. People being healed, canes being nailed to the walls, and terminally ill people reporting FULL recoveries.

Elder Bass would sit me on his lap and teach me the Bible pretty much like Elder Ross; only Elder Bass would throw in a joke or two to make me laugh. This made learning about God even more interesting to me.

Elder Melvin Bass (November 20, 1924 - January 8, 2005) and Mother Dorothy Bass

EPIPHANY

Mother Dorothy Bass, Elder Melvin's wife, was very strict with the Word of God as well! She would often quiz me by starting a Bible verse and then ask me, "What does the rest of the scripture say?" I even remember one time, one of their grandsons was in trouble and about to be punished. She asked him, "Do you know what the Bible says about sparing the rod?" He answered, "Yes, Ma'am." And he proceeded to quote the whole scripture! "He that spareth his rod hateth his son: but he that loveth him chasteneth him betimes." (Proverbs 13:24). Mother Bass just laughed. Lol! Well, he didn't get punished that day. God's Grace is sufficient, and the Word still works!

Being a great grill master himself, Elder Bass made his home a popular spot to stop and receive tons of love from the beautiful brick BBQ pit he made himself. I can still smell the savory smoke of his well-seasoned summer delights. Thank you, Bass Family, for the beautiful memories.

MARSHON PEOPLES

# BULLET FIVE

Being raised in the church, I often found my comfort in the scriptures of the Holy Bible. I remember when I stumbled upon 1 Peter 2:4-10 with the key verse being verse 9:

## 1 Peter 2:4-10

> But ye are a chosen generation, a royal priesthood, a holy nation, a peculiar people; that ye should shew forth the praises of Him who hath called you out of darkness into His marvelous light

This gave me the most comfort, not knowing that this particular scripture would eventually manifest naturally and spiritually in my life. Specifically, Friday, January 6, 2012, when I'm introduced to the Designated Bullet I call Epiphany, and my life flashes before my eyes:

*I hear a BOOM! Then... darkness... I can't see. I can't move. I feel like I'm floating. I can't hear anything... Oh! There's a sound... faint pop-like sound in the distance... Are they still shooting? Lord, not like this... not like this... Is this it? Is this how I'm about to go?...*

I had another childhood friend named Eric Cannon; we called him "Boogie." I don't know why the nickname. But Eric was 7, he and I played together every chance we got. After church we would plead with our parents to spend the night at each other's homes. Eric and I played Batman and Robin—all... the ...time. He was always Batman, and, me being younger, I would accept being Robin.

We would swing around the poles of the basement of Eric's house, leaping from toy box to couch to washing machine, imagining that we were leaping from rooftop to rooftop. We fought the imaginary characters of Joker, Penguin, and Riddler. With our mouths, we made our own sound effects, pausing with each swing as we waited for our comic blurb bubble to appear: "POW!", "BANG!", "OUCH!", "OOF!", "WACK!" We were the Dynamic Duo!

Eric even taught me how to ride a bike! He had a small, red two-wheeler Schwinn-style bike with a banana seat and no training wheels. His bike was small enough for me to put my feet on the ground while I was on it, but I couldn't ride it yet. I would run and chase Eric while he was on it. Lol... we had so much fun!

# EPIPHANY

One day Eric told me, "Get on!" I replied, "But I can't ride." Eric was very persuasive. He laughed, "You can learn... I'll teach you!" He continued, "Get on! Put your feet on both sides..." I really wanted to ride. My friend and tutor assured me, "I will hold the bike and you pedal." We would try and try again, but I couldn't keep the bike balanced. I didn't understand the concept that "motion" is what balanced people. Oops, I mean the bike. 😁 Everyday, he tried to help me to ride.

Finally, one day we were playing outside, having fun as usual. I was sitting on the bike, although I still wasn't riding it properly. I would sit on it, run like the Flintstones, and pick my feet up once I gained some momentum. Lol Eric noticed and yelled, "Shon! Just put your feet on the pedals!" And I did! Eric seemed happier than I was as he ran alongside me with excitement, shouting, "You're riding, you're riding!!!!" Like the movie *Forest Gump*. I was riding!

Just then, Eric's father (Min. Michael Cannon) came home and saw me on the bike, and he yelled, "Get that boy off that bike before he fall!!!" Eric says back "But Dad, he can ride now, see!" Just then, much to my dismay, I fell.

It took some time after that "fall" to prove to his dad I could ride a bike. He just didn't want me to get hurt under his watch. But at least I knew for myself... "I can now ride a bike." And I want one of my own.

Whether selfish or unselfish in nature, the rule remains the same: the older ones teach the younger ones. Eric was also very good with the Bible. He could find scriptures really fast. You see, at Messias Temple in those days, the first person to find the scripture Pastor Ross mentioned in Bible class would start reading. In most cases Eric would find the scriptures even before the adults! Pastor Ross and the others ministers and elders would marvel at Eric's knowledge of where the scriptures were located. He would read them loud and clear.

During one particular Bible class, when a well-known speaker, Robert Evans, was visiting, Eric was being Eric, finding scriptures left and right. Robert Evans would laugh every time Eric would find the scripture and read them with such authority! After service, a crowd of people stood around Eric with praises and accolades.

# EPIPHANY

I remember asking Eric at the age of 6, "How do you find the scriptures so fast?" Eric answered, "It's because I have the Holy Ghost and you don't!" True to my childish nature, I responded, "Well, I've been baptized in Jesus' Name!" Eric came back with even more strength in his voice. "That's only one part; you need the Holy Ghost too!" I stood silent with no answer when Eric added, "I have the Spirit of God in me—the Holy Ghost—and you don't!"

I believe, to this day, what I looked up to wasn't the fact that he could find the scriptures quickly, nor that he received high accolades, nor that he was older than me and seemed to be good at everything, but the fact that he had the same promise made unto Abraham that Pastor Ross had shared with me, the same promise God wanted to give to me. "Eric got it, and I don't?!" Well, I wanted it too. Plus, I was tired of being Robin

MARSHON PEOPLES

# BULLET SIX

# EPIPHANY

On October 30, 1980, when I was 6 years old, our church experienced a revival. A woman named Sister Naomi Cesly was in town. She is what we call a "birth mother." A birth mother is someone who understands her purpose in administering the preparation of the heart, so God can give His gift, i.e., The Holy Ghost, to His chosen. This was a true revival. The Spirit of the Lord was thick in the atmosphere. I'm not talking about the fast music, people singing and running around kind of atmosphere. There was this powerful quietness about the place.

Sister Cesly asked the congregation, "Who here wants something from the Lord?" I sat there in my seat next to my mother, feeling like Sister Cesly was speaking directly to me. The spiritual pull was so very strong. Sister Cesly says, "If you seek something from God, now is the time." At this point, my heart felt like it was beating a mile a minute. I felt as if God Himself was standing at the front of the church with His arms wide open. I tapped my mother and said, "I want the Holy Ghost." I believe my mother was so into the service that she didn't want to miss anything pertaining to what God was doing that night.

She must have figured I was just talking about something unrelated to the message. She kind of waved me off as if to say, "Sit back and be quiet."

I knew well enough not to be bad in church from previous experiences of "not sitting back and being quiet" if you all know what I mean. I know my backside remembers all too well! But this was different; I could feel the spiritual pull even more, so I took the risk and tapped my mother again and said, "I want the Holy Ghost." I thought my mother might take me downstairs to the storage closet and give me a really good "backside experience" again, but she didn't. This time she says, "Go tell Sister Walton."

Now, Sister Walton was a good friend of my mother's. And I liked her a lot because she and her husband, Floyd, were always so nice to me. Sister Walton was sitting a few pews in front of my mother and me. So I made my way up to Sister Walton. She was sitting on the end, close to the aisle where I was walking. Her elbow was on the armrest. I touched her arm, leaned my face toward her and said, "Sister Walton? I want the Holy Ghost." She looked at me, smiled a big smile, and said, "Let's go."

## EPIPHANY

She stood up, took my hand, and walked me up to the front of the church where Sister Cesly was standing. Sister Cesly leaned down and greeted me with a hug. Then she asked me, "What is it that you want from the Lord?" I replied to her, "I want the Holy Ghost." Cesly responds back, "Do you know what the Holy Ghost is?" I replied again, "Yes, it is the Spirit of God, and I want Him inside me."

It was as if time stood still. I heard nothing else around me but Cesly. Cesly whispered softly into my ear, "Think of the goodness of Jesus, all the good that has happened to you is from Him. Now, I want you to open your mouth and drink these words..." She said, "He that believeth on Jesus, as the scripture hath said, out of his belly shall flow rivers of living water which is the Holy Ghost, which they that believe on Him should receive." (St. John 7:38, 39).

Cesly continued to speak softly in my mouth and ear, quoting St. John 7:38, 39, Acts 2:1-4 and Acts 2:38. Cesly said, "Yes, that's it. Drink the Word of God, don't be afraid; something will begin to happen... Just let it happen." I will never forget the experience. I took deep breaths as she spoke. I thought of everything good I could think of. My knees and my stomach began to quiver.

My lips and mouth began to vibrate. I still heard Cesly speaking and quoting scriptures into my mouth, some of the same scriptures Pastor Jesse Ross had shown me in prior Bible classes. I believed every word she spoke, as she quoted the Word of God.

Then suddenly... it was like an eruption!! Words I did not understand just flowed out of my mouth. The words came and moved swiftly from across my tongue. Tears streamed down my face. My mouth was moving rapidly and I was allowing it to happen. I felt like I couldn't get all that was in me out fast enough. I began bobbing up and down, bending at the knees, trying to stop my body from quivering. My mouth felt funny, like a soft sweet tickle in the back of my throat. The words continued to flow from me. I heard nothing else around me but these unknown words.

I didn't even hear Sister Cesly at this point. It was wonderful! Powerful! Excellent! I felt like God Himself was hugging me. No... more like I was engulfed in Him. Him being as to some Jesus Christ, YAHuSHAuAH (I AM Salvation Almighty) Ha' Mishiach in Hebrew or, in other words, The Messiah. I was speaking with other tongues, as the Spirit, the Holy Ghost gave me utterance!

EPIPHANY

After some time, my mouth finally stopped moving. I remember sitting on the very front pew of the church, feeling fresh. My body was exhausted, and my mouth still had that soft funny tickle feeling in the back. Pastor Jesse Ross was standing on the pulpit behind the podium with a microphone in his hand. He had someone bring me up there to him. It seemed so high being up there on the pulpit, looking down at everyone's faces of surety, smiles, and some full of wonder. Their faces looked at me as if I had become a part of something bigger than all of us, which they had experienced the same as I had in their previous, respective due seasons.

Pastor Ross then spoke to me through the microphone so that everyone in the church could hear. He spoke with that strong, deep, slow voice as he asked me, "Do you know what you have?" I replied to him with tears of joy, unspeakable, crying out, "I got the Holy Ghost!" I began speaking those unknown words again, and I couldn't seem to stop. The words began echoing throughout the sanctuary. The church erupted into a crazed frenzy of praise to God. People were all over, worshiping, shouting, clapping, honoring, and magnifying the Name of Jesus.

I could see this frothy white haze hovering towards the top of the sanctuary. God was definitely in that place that night, and He came to give me the precious gift of The Holy Ghost. The *Ruach Ha'Kodesh* in Hebrew, which, directly translated, means "the breath of the Whole One." I am now truly a living soul.

From that time onward, numerous protections and provisions have been granted to me by God—my Heavenly Father and Friend—despite my limited understanding of how He orchestrates events. Nevertheless, He has consistently accompanied me throughout my life.

EPIPHANY

# BULLET SEVEN

The day after experiencing the Holy Ghost, my mother granted me permission to attend the University of Michigan football game with my elder godbrother, Carlitos Bostic (Carl). I was filled with excitement! You couldn't have given me a greater gift after receiving the Holy Ghost! I went to the game with Carl, Antoinette and Bernadette, Carl's younger twin sisters—my god-family.

It was so cold that day, but I didn't care. I sat between the twins to stay warm. We huddled under a blanket as the Wolverine players huddled on the field. Carl was working as a vendor that day at the Big House. He was a freshman but would soon be playing in games himself. It was great to just be spending time with friends and family, especially with my god-bro, Carlitos Bostic, aka Dawg 99... "Big strong, fast, everybody knows him." He was and still is like a superhero to me.

After all that had just transpired, I didn't feel like Robin anymore. I felt more like Superman! In remembering times past, I realize I always seemed to encounter bullies as a child.

EPIPHANY

And to be honest, most kids seemed different than me. They all talked differently and walked differently that me. I often got the sense that they thought they were better than me Hence, the cruel name-calling in reference to my name and whatever else they could use to single me out.

Three brothers lived on the same street as my mother and me during our time on Adams Street. I recall the youngest brother's name was Ri Ri. The three brothers constantly found a reason to mess with me by taking my things and beating me up and laugh about it. I often confided in some of my friends on the block, only to learn that they were also afraid of the three stooges! Some of the kids would join the three brothers in scrutinizing me in hopes that they would be left alone.

I remember my mom telling me, "Don't come in this house NOT ONE MORE TIME crying that somebody hit you!" She went on to say, "If you have to, you take something and cold cock them, or you gonna get a WHOOPIN'! Do you hear me?!" My mom could really yell. But it wasn't so much the yelling that got to me; it was the fact that if I lost the fight ... *I* was getting a WHOOPIN'?

Wait, if he beat me up, I get whooped? I was more afraid of my mom than anyone else, so I thought, "I'd better win." I get it. As a single mother, she didn't want me to be afraid since she wouldn't always be around.

Oh, by the way, Pastor Jesse Ross stayed at the other end of our street. I remember one particular day, I went down to Pastor Ross's house and began speaking to him about the three brothers. Pastor Ross leaned forward in his rocking chair, which sat on the front porch of his house, and said to me in that deep, slow voice of his, "Did you pray?" I replied, "No, Elder Ross." He leaned backward in his rocking chair and said, "Well, then you go pray, and I'll pray, then we will see what the Lord says about it."

I remember standing there purely distraught. I thought maybe he would talk to the boys or call some brothers from the church to handle this. I expected something different from what I got. Pastor Ross only stayed the fourth house down from me, but that walk home seemed long and lonely. I didn't feel too "super" at the time. On top of that, to my dismay, who do I see walking toward me? The youngest of the three brothers... Ri Ri.

# EPIPHANY

I ran as fast as I could to get inside my house before he could do anything to me. Whew! I made it, but he was still standing outside my house! Ri Ri was standing on the sidewalk in front of my living room window, waving at me with a crooked, mischievous smile. He even came and started peering in the window to see if he could get a better look at me.

This made me so angry!!! I remember thinking, "Why won't they just leave me alone?!" So, I went and got my big... red... wide... plastic WIFFLE ball bat out of my toy box. And I waited for Ri Ri to start walking away. As he did... I ran out of my house, caught up to Ri Ri, and began hitting him—"cold cocking," as my mom would say—as many times as I could with my WIFFLE ball bat! Oooh, it felt so good to get Ri Ri back for everything he did to me.

His two older brothers must have heard Ri Ri's screams. I heard the screen door to their house slam shut.... "WACK!" It was like a starter pistol of an Olympic race. At least, for me, it was! I dropped my WIFFLE ball bat and ran as fast as my lil' legs would carry me. I heard the two older brothers yell out, "We gon' get you!" I don't think I ever ran so fast! It was like I made it back to my house, inside, door shut and locked in 1 second flat! I felt good, but only for a moment. I thought, "What am I gonna do now? I probably won't ever be able to go back outside... They have my WIFFLE ball bat!" And my final thought was, "I should have prayed... I wonder, is it too late?" At the age of 6, I kneeled down and prayed my first real prayer. Before, I used to pray the lil' cutesy prayer, which starts with "Now I lay me down to sleep…" This prayer was different, though—it was from my heart. It was real to me because I felt I really needed God's help.

My Aunt Sherita was home at the time. She didn't know what I had just done. I remember her asking me, "What's wrong, Shon?" I was on my knees, and I replied, "Nothing, just praying." "Good for you Shon!" she responded, and then kept busy with whatever she was working on. I couldn't believe what I had just done. I didn't play outside much after that, unless it was at Pastor Ross' house or Eric's house, which was in Ann Arbor. But God surely does answer prayers.

EPIPHANY

I don't remember how much longer after my prayer it was, but at some point, those three brothers moved away, and I haven't seen them since. Lol! Amen. (Count how many times the word "pray" was mentioned in this testimony.)

MARSHON PEOPLES

# BULLET EIGHT

EPIPHANY

I can remember another one of the Lord's protections from when I was in the first grade at George Elementary School. I missed the bus trying to give my friend, Jeff, his paper to give to his parents, as the teacher had told me to do. Jeff kept running as I called out to him, and I couldn't catch up to him. I turned to catch my own bus, only to see it pulling off from the school. I ran back to the school, but all the doors I checked were locked. I didn't know what to do.

I started walking in what I believed to be the direction of Elder and Sister Ross's house, which was where I was supposed to be. I said, "God, I know You're with me because I have the Holy Ghost." I made up my mind to walk to where I knew I needed to be... Just then, the bus driver came back and got me safely to my destination. Amen.

The Lord even blessed me in school! A specific memory comes to mind from when I was in the first grade at George Elementary. I was doing my math problems, and sitting next to me was someone who is still a great friend of mine today, Nyree Swanson.

As I was sitting next to her, I noticed that my math problems looked different than hers. Mine had a plus (+) and minus sign (-), and hers had a sideways plus sign (x) and a minus sign with two dots, one above and one below (÷). Lol. Mind you, I was in the first grade. I asked her, "What is that?" She said, "This is multiplication."

Nyree had a third-grade math book in the first grade. I responded, "A multiplication, what's that?" She began to show me. She said, "Okay, multiplication is when you have like three fingers, and then you add another three fingers. How much is that?" she asked like she was my tutor. I said, "Six." "Now add another three fingers," she instructed. "1, 2, 3, 4," I counted with my fingers, then said, "9!" excitedly. "So, how many sets of three do you see?" she asked. I answered, "It's like three!" "So 3 x 3 = 9," she explained. "That's multiplication!" I've been in love with math ever since. Thank you, Nyree!

## Hint to Understand Math

> Math is absolute. Meaning it's always constant and never changes. 2 + 2 always = 4. Follow every step in a math problem, and it will give you the answer.

And God blessed them, and God said unto them, Be fruitful, and multiply, and replenish the earth, and subdue it: and have dominion over the fish of the sea, and over the fowl of the air, and over every living thing that moveth upon the earth. ~ Genesis 1:28

As a matter of fact, around the same time, in the second grade, I can remember they had me in some special class. I remember telling my mom, "It's boring in there." They had me reading stuff like, "See Jan ran." and "See Spot and Jan ran." Keep in mind, Elder Ross was reading me the Bible at that time. So, "See Jan ran." had nothing on "Taste and see that the LORD is good." The Kingdom.

After I told my mom about my class at school, she was so mad. I thought I'd done something wrong! I remember she brought me up to the school, kind of snatching my arm and everything as we went to the principal's office. I remember sitting in the main office and can hear my mom fussing inside the office with the principal of my school. The door was shut. Needless to say, she got me out of that special ed class. Amen.

EPIPHANY

# BULLET NINE

A nother blessing of the Lord was when I got a chance to go with the church to SeaWorld! We had a group at our church called The Messias Temple Boys and Girls Club. It was so much fun! I remember staying up most of the night before the outing—I could barely get any sleep. I kept waking up and wondering, "Did I miss my ride?!" I sat there looking out my bedroom window, waiting and waiting as the darkness turned to light, as the morning sun was just about to rise. Sitting there, arms folded, face planted, staring out the window, waiting for the church van to arrive. When it finally came, I was so happy I hadn't missed it.

It was a long ride to get to SeaWorld, but well worth it. There were so many sea animals and other sites to see that I had never seen in person before. I also remember a special event with a famous dog named Boomer. What an intelligent dog! He could do all kinds of tricks. I was sitting on the far end of the front row, enjoying every minute of the show! Suddenly, the MC asked for a volunteer. I raise my hand as most kids would when somebody asks, "May I have a volunteer?" To my excitement, the MC selected me! I walked all the way up to that long stage situated outdoors —amphitheater style—and met my favorite dog, Boomer.

The MC instructed me to tell Boomer to pick out a few articles of clothing that were upstairs in an old pirate ship that was on the stage. He told me to tell the dog in his ear. I thought the MC meant his own ear, so I whispered in the MC's ear, "A shirt." The MC replied, "Not in my ear; the dog's ear!" The crowd laughed hysterically.

So, I whispered in the dog's ear to go get a tie. Boomer ran up and came back with a tie—just what I had asked for! The MC asked if this was what I asked for. I said, "Yes! That's what I asked for!" Everybody clapped. Next, I asked Boomer for a shirt. He ran to the room and came back out as before, this time with a bra!!! I was so embarrassed. The MC said, "Young man, what kind of mind do you have on you?" I think I spent the whole day trying to explain to people I asked for a shirt, not a bra. The church members laughed and joked with me. I was pleading my case with each jester, "I asked for a shirt, not a bra!"

Anyway, they gave me a nice pen that said "Boomers Buddy" on it. So that's just another fond memory I have and another major thing that the God I serve has done for me. Young and full of the Holy Ghost, with some wonderful experiences. And more was yet to come.

It wasn't all about receiving blessings, being provided for, or receiving protections. Abba also used me, as the Holy Ghost within, in some ways too! I can remember speaking with my friend, Wayne, and he had done something that he wasn't supposed to do. I told him, "Tell the truth." and he's like, "What if I tell the truth and I get a whooping?!" I told him, "Yeah, you might get a whooping, but at least it won't be as bad because you told the truth." So, apparently, he must have gone home and told the truth because his mother brought him over to our apartment. We all stayed in Camelot Apartments in Ypsilanti.

My mom answered the door, kind of frowning like, "What has happened," or, "What has Shon done now?" As she opened the door, standing there was my friend Wayne and his gorgeous mom, a tall, blonde-haired woman with blue eyes. She looked like someone you would see in a Vogue Magazine (or an Instagram video for those who need a more contemporary reference). Wayne's Dad was a dark-skinned, cool brother like a Shaft or Chadwick Boseman, aka Black Panther.

EPIPHANY

Wayne's mom said, "Doris, I want to thank you. I want to thank you for how you raised your son because he told my son to tell the truth, and he can play with my son anytime he wants!" I did encourage him to tell the truth, but that was the Holy Ghost! The Lord used His Spirit through me to help others. There are still even more mysteries to come.

I remember when our church, Messias Temple, recorded a choir album! It was so exciting!!! We were recording at a church on Eastern Michigan University's campus because our church at the time was too small. It was a packed house!!! And the songs we recorded are timeless. The singers and musicians were phenomenal! You might as well say our whole church was the choir—everyone full of talent.

I was baptized in the melodic music of Sister Bass. What stands out to me is when she would sing out her prayers in tongues—simply beautiful. Other singers who come to mind are Hattie Smith, Stephanie Rose Smith, Maretta Smith, Michael Swanigan, Brenda Dixon Bird, Henry "Butch" Frost... the list goes on and on. But one person in particular would sing in such a way that heaven would open in response to her sound: the late, great Geraldine Whitman.

You'll agree if you get your hands on Messias Temple's album. As you can see, I was raised in music. If you do happen to look them up: enjoy!

Messias Temple Choir Album Cover (front)

Messias Temple Choir Album Choir (back)

# EPIPHANY

Evangelist YVONNE HAWKINS
Mistress of Ceremony

Messias Temple Choir Album Recording Service

Broderick Cannon (Percussion) & Henry "Butch" Frost
(The Baddest Left-Handed Bass Player)

Out of this wonderful choir came a sensational group called Inspiration. I used to get excited as a kid when I saw the microphones at the front of the little Messias Temple church with the yellow, red, blue and orange sponge guards on them. I knew we were in for a treat that night! This group had a lot of the people from the choir—I believe some of the best: Brenda, Debbie, Derrick, Henry, Mr. Chip Sr., Russell, Fabian, and Kiera. They would sing songs like "Satisfied" and, my favorite, "Do You Really Love the Lord."

I will say, though, Willie Walker and Annette Wilson had those of us who were in Messias Temple Youth Choir some years later, sounding good too! As you can see, I was raised in music.

Thank you all for your worship.

EPIPHANY

# BULLET TEN

# I Corinthians 13:11

> When I was a child, I spoke as a child, I understood as a child, I thought as a child; but when I became a man, I put away childish things.

My adolescent and teenage years were filled with many changes. Changes like friends, styles, music, and interests like sports! I remember in the sixth grade, the school—Estabrook Elementary—was hosting a field day event. One of the challenges was a relay race. I can't remember who ran the lead, but I was second leg, Hasun Patterson ran third, and Jermanie Williams ran anchor. The other teams were talented as well, if not more. One of the other teams was really stacked. They had Robert Addie and D. Smitty. Even then, both of them were some fast runners, who, in later years, I would play high school football with.

I looked around to see my competition. We were evenly matched in my mind, and I was thinking, "Just run as hard as I can." You see, my leg of the race was in the bend of the

EPIPHANY

track. Because of this, it appeared as if some of the other opponents were ahead of me, so I thought it was unfair, but I had to catch the first person in my leg. Lol!

The race began: "On your marks, get set, GO!" I watched as my teammate got closer. I remembered the gym teacher telling the class as we were learning to run a relay race, "Start running before your teammate gets to you."

So, as my teammate got close, I started running, but not at full speed til I got the stick… I got it! Now to catch the first person in my leg, which was David Norton, but David didn't have his stick yet. I let loose to get there when he got his stick. He got it, and we were tied neck and neck in the bend of the track… or so I thought.

As we approached the straightaway on the track, I saw that we were in the lead!!! Now I really ran my hardest because I didn't want David to catch us. Lol! I handed the stick off to Hasun Patterson, and he increased the lead even further! Now our anchor was no slouch by any stretch of the imagination. Jermanie was fast! Hasun handed off to Jermanie, and he took off. We were dusting everyone! No one was even close. But then Jermanie saw how big of a lead we had and slowed down to this "peacockish" slow jog as if to say, "We got this," or "Like taking candy from a baby." Lol.

Well, D. Smitty got his stick. I don't know what was on Smitty's mind, but his afterburner was blazing behind him… lol, because he was coming fast and gaining on my teammate. I yelled while flailing my arm to signal him to RUUUUUNNN!!!!

Jermanie was like one of those people in the movies who just don't see the trouble right behind them. He waved at me like, "Hi, yes, we're winning. Feels good, huh? Yeah, we got this." But we didn't. By the time Jermanie noticed D. Smitty running, knees high, at top speed, with every intention of catching up to him, it was too late. Jermanie couldn't crank up his legs to his top speed fast enough to hold off the momentum of our competitor, who was already in the "flow."

So yes, we lost. However, I learned from Smitty never to give up. Smitty would continue this mentality throughout

EPIPHANY

academics, sports, and other accomplishments. We may fall, but we learn to get back up. Thank you for your example of strength. D Smitty currently owns a Daycare with his family called Extraordinary Individuals. ~ Blessings

Moral of the story: Don't quit because you win. Don't quit because you lose. Get better at your talent. Then, look for ways to earn a living doing what you love. I am here to help (www.GoodePeoples.com).

MARSHON PEOPLES

# BULLET ELEVEN

# EPIPHANY

I mostly hang out with friends from church. Around sixth grade I began to realize there's a huge difference between going to church and living for God. My questions about salvation grew as well. I found myself buried in the Bible. I searched for answers to my own shortcomings all the time. Between playing basketball, drawing, singing, and songwriting, I was most confident with my now best friend, Robert Lucas (Bo). Eric no longer attended the same church as I did, so we grew apart. Robert and I met in the fifth grade at a barbeque held at the house of one of the members of our church—Evangelist Yvonne Hawkins (she later became Pastor Hawkins-Bell).

I remember Bo was still in the car playing with his toys. I went to ask his Mom (Evangelist Debbie Lucas) if he would like to play with the other kids and me. She replied, "You can try. See if he'll come out of that car." So I went and knocked on the window of their car. He ignored me. I knocked on the window again, and he continued to ignore me (Lol). I said, "Hey, you want to come out and play with us?" He ignored me, still again, as he played with some of his He-Man action figures. I finally walked away and went back to the front porch of the house, continually looking back to their car into the backseat window of their little gray

Chevette as he continued his solo imaginary play. All of a sudden, he came out of the car and joined us! He and I have been friends ever since. There was even a short time when I went to Edmondson Middle School—the same school he attended. He and I would jump in the air and high-five whenever we saw each other in the hallway, like in a hoop game. Lol!

This was also around the time I got better at basketball, when the Granthams stayed down the street from me on Chevrolet. I stayed on the Willow Run side of Tyler on Calder. I loved football, but the Granthams mostly played basketball. So I played with their grandchildren Nate "Pow" Griffin II, (currently owner of Hungry Hustla Gym) and Jeron Currie (currently owns a commercial cleaning company), and sometimes with some of the others like David and Chris Grantham. If you are around this family, two things will happen... you're going to eat extremely well and learn to play basketball! Thanks, Grantham family!

A special memory of Papa Cornelius Grantham: He had been staying in the hospital, and my mom said, "Papa Grantham would love to see you." He wasn't really remembering many people at this time, so I was nervous. I didn't want him to not remember me. But a warm feeling comes over me right now as I remember coming into his room. He immediately smiled and said, "Shon." Thank you, Papa Grantham, for all you ever did for me.

In the same way, my mother, being the woman of God that she was, said, "Let's take some flowers to Mother Catherine Grantham." I got excited! "Yes," I said, "Let's go pick out some really pretty ones too!" We went to St Joe to visit Mother Grantham. Lois—one of Mother Grantham's daughters—and Mother Grantham's grandchildren were already there, and I put the flowers in front of my face so she didn't know it was me. When I removed the flowers from my face, she smiled that wonderful womanly smile of hers and said," Shon?! Hey, y'all, this my son right here." In front of everybody in the hospital room. Thank you, Mama Grantham for everything you've ever done for me. Love you very much.

Thank you to ALL the Granthams for sharing them both with me. Bo and I had so much in common: art, drawing, music, video games, you name it. This made us become close very quickly. Our difference was our temperament. He would get mad quickly, while it takes a lot to make me angry. However, he would get over it quickly and say, "skip it," whereas, on the other hand, when I got mad... I was mad for old stuff *and* new stuff! I would be mad at stuff someone else had done, and I would unleash all my anger on my current target, the entity that made me mad... person, place or thing (waxed hot! lol).

Our differences balanced us out, and our closeness is mainly because we were both the only children in our households. The difference is Bo's father and mother are married and together to this day. Bo's father is a strong man who supports his family. Favorably for me, Robert's father became a father figure in my life. I love his take-charge attitude toward everything he does. I admired his thinking mind. I challenged him often over the years in chess. I still haven't won a game against him (lol). My confidence in becoming a man came from watching him and a few other men who attended our church.

Men like:
Ralph Johnson, the fun man in the church. Ralph is the guy that every time you're with him, you are going to have fun, eat at a delicious restaurant, learn the Word, and get advice and laughter by the ton. He would also ask questions to

help me come to a better understanding of my situation over the years.

Tom Caddell, the handyman. We called him "Top." It seemed like Top could fix anything. Car, house, bike, plumbing, cement, bricklaying etc… I could go on, but you get it. He was a "renaissance man." He would come get me to work on the construction sites and play with his son, Tarrance. I learned a lot from him. Thank you, Pastor Ivy Caddell, for sharing him with me and feeding me with your delicious, southern-style meals.

Keith "Big Poppa" Toney, the sharp-dressing, great-smelling worship leader. He and his family are all singers! From him and his gorgeous, soft-spoken wife, Reverna, to his three beautiful girls and his son—my friend—Kevin Toney. Keith is an archetype of the word "father." He has this regal posture of respect yet kindness. He leads worship in a way that ushers in the presence of God and makes me surrender totally to my Savior.

His son Kevin and I became close. We even sang together in the choir and in a group we formed called Dominion. Kevin is also the nephew of Karl Reid, a singing member of the phenom gospel group called Commissioned.

William Lundy, the most tempered man I knew. Mr. Bill, as we often called him, was my most influential Sunday school teacher. He could draw extremely well. One time he drew me! And it looked like a black-and-white photo to me.

Mr. Bill would teach us the Bible in a way that the young people could understand. I would sit and listen to his Vietnam stories. This is why I say he is the most-tempered man. After all that he had been through and was capable of, he was always calm. As a matter of fact, he was only excited when magnifying our God! His words, "Don't try; DO!" Always stuck with me. Thank you, Mr. Bill!

Derrick Thomas, the coolest man in the church. And that's saying a lot! Many men in this congregation were cool, each with their own strengths. But Derrick had a swag, with a tall 6'4" to 6'6" slim frame and long strides as he walked that caused him to sway and look smooth while he did it.

He has a beautiful wife, Teresa, two daughters my age, and a younger son. The ideal look of coolness. Minister Norman

Wilson, the dynamic preacher. The cool on him is strong too! An amazing drummer, and the way he treats his wife is awesome! He would get in his car after church and pull up close to the door to wait for her. She would come out and get in the car, and they would sit a little longer in the parking lot.

One day I asked Min. Wilson, "What are you doing when you two sit in the car?" He replied with a cool grin, "We share what we learned from God today, and the rest is none of your business." I laughed immediately and made it my own. His beloved sister was our long-time Youth Choir Director and friend—the late, great Annette Wilson.

Brad Holman. He mentored my friends and me in the Bible, basketball, ideas, and community. Every so often, we would go with him to the hoop courts on a Saturday, and we'd shut down court after court. It became the norm. Brad would orchestrate us as a team on the court, teaching us the art of the game. Everyone knew him. He also seemed to know everyone and was always ready to lend them a helping hand.

Carlitos Bostic is my big God brother. My protector, advisor, and just a great guy. He is a big, strong former University of Michigan linebacker and played for a few pro teams. And he is hilarious! Always had us laughing, especially on the church bus trips to other churches and events.

Henry "Butch" Frost, a family man of God with eight children. Undoubtedly the baddest bass player around! He has the ability to play a right-handed bass upside down with his left hand. Oh, did I mention he's left-handed?

That gives him a sound that I believe few people can achieve. He has a beautiful wife, Kina "Madea" Frost, who will feed you emotionally, spiritually, and of course, naturally, too! I ate many great meals and laughed a lot. This is a family of a million laughs.

My boy Charles "Prazm Bruh" ("Praise Him Brother") Marshall, a researcher, and lover of God. He and I would talk about the Bible for hours. We would see the same things in the Bible but from different standpoints. Just cool to hang out with as well. Frank "Chucky" James, aka Big Frank, a big bro of mine (owner of Good Eats Food Truck (www.GoodEats.biz).

He's closer to my age but a protector of mine nonetheless. He helped me with football, weights, and a lil' street knowledge. I can remember being jumped by some boys after my football game when one of my teammates, Shadrick, picked me up from behind from out of the center of my scrum. I thought I was done for sure because I didn't know who had me. Shadrick then put me in Frank's car.

Frank was already cheesing and laughed, "What you doin' fightin'?" I laughed back, but little did he know I had been in those situations before. However, I was happy he was there. By this time, Pastor Elder Jesse Ross had transitioned, and a new pastor was installed—Elder Harry S. Grayson. Pastor Grayson is a former youth leader—a favorite of ours—turned pastor.

Bishop Grayson of P.A.W.—previously Pastor Grayson—is also a friend. His focus is more on higher education, hard work, diligence, and dedication. Don't let the smooth exterior fool you, though; he is also very funny and whimsical. And don't engage him for a Dozens battle, because you *will* lose! Lol!

Bishop Grayson used to come get me when I was little too! He would take me on different trips and let me ride on his motorcycle. He and Elder N. Grantham helped me develop a work ethic, starting with raking leaves and cutting grass. Bishop Grayson was one of the reasons I started a newspaper route. One day he came to get me to rake some leaves behind his house. I had never seen so many leaves! It was insane!!! So I was out there raking by myself. I only had a rake, and I was just a raking… one bag, two bags, three bags… I must have gotten up to maybe four or five bags of leaves, and I still had tons more leaves to go, before

he came out and said, "You ain't done yet? You're too slow!" Then he laughed that laugh of his.

## Golden Nugget

So what he did was he got the lawn mower and started mowing my mountain pile of leaves up into the lawn mower bag and then bagged it from the lawn mower bag in minutes.

And then told my mother and others he did most of the work! Well, he did because he had a smarter way. Well, after seeing that, I stopped raking leaves because I had nowhere to store a lawn mower at my mom's apartment in Camelot. So that's why I went and got a paper route like my friend, Bo. Lol!

The fact that my big brother, Carl, attended the University of Michigan and Pastor Harry Grayson, at that time, worked at the same university, were the reasons why I felt a strong pull to want to attend the institution later in life. They were also the reasons I wanted to pursue higher learning. And yeah, I wanted to make my mentors proud.

Thank you, Bishop Grayson, for all the years of service, sacrifice, tutelage, example, leadership, friendship, laughter, and, more importantly, what God gave you concerning His Word. Amen. ~ Blessings.

Pastor Grayson's preaching style is full of practical applications of the Word of God with mostly parables and analogies to give us better understanding like our Savior did in the Bible.

MARSHON PEOPLES

## "If you do what I do, you can get what I got."
## Bishop Harry S. Grayson

I was more used to Elder Bass (Nov 20, 1924 – Jan 8, 2005) and Elder Ross staying within "walking the book" so I gravitated to Elder Larry Clifton more.

Elder Larry Clifton
(September 29, 1950 – August 31, 2023)

# EPIPHANY

Elder Clifton is my best friend's uncle and my hero. When no one else could answer my questions concerning the Bible, he could and would in the mightiest way. He would be ready with an answer. Whereas, when other men in the church would try to answer my questions, they would sometimes leave me with even more questions. Other than Elder Melvin Bass, Elder Clifton was the only one who would take me straight to the Word of God and say, "read."

At the age of 17, I would come to his home quite often and ask just one question. This true man of God would sit with me from 3pm to 3am, answering my one question using only the Word of God, while answering hundreds of other questions I would have asked at the same time. We would go to a scripture and he'd say, "God said what? Now read." Then say, "Why did God say it? Continue... read." Pretty much like Pastor Elder Jesse Ross did when I was younger.

Elder Clifton continued to train me to "walk the book" or, in other words, how to truly read, study and rightly divide the Bible. He would expound on words like "if," "for," "therefore," "unto," "until," "so," etc. These words would give God's Word order, understanding, meaning, clarity, and purpose. I no longer had to guess what God's Word meant; I simply had to ask God for understanding and keep reading.

One day in church, Elder Clifton came to me and said, "Shon I need you to draw me something." This was nothing strange to me; many ministers were always asking me to draw one thing or another. So I said, "Sure!" Elder Clifton said, "I want you to draw me a Bible with a flame coming out of it, and I want all these scriptures to be incorporated throughout the drawing." So I did the drawing for him.

"This is POWERFUL!" he said. He wasn't speaking about my drawing ability per se. You see, it was a simple drawing. However, I had run out of room on the page and had two more words to incorporate into the drawing. The only other place I could fit anything would be in the flame, coming out of the open Bible. The two words that were left were "Spirit" and "Baptism," which were both incorporated into the flame. His next response was, "Flesh and blood didn't reveal this to you, man."

At the time, I was naïve to what I had drawn that this profound man in the Word of God would be so excited about. It was his main message. The Spirit of evangelism regarding, i.e., Ecclesia, Paracletos, Ruach HaKodesh, otherwise known as the Holy Ghost, unlocked the understanding of "End-Time Prophecy," which he had written a book about.

There were other men I observed and learned from, from afar, like my late Uncle Monroe "June" Peoples Jr. (rested in the Lord July in 2022) and Uncle Donzell Peoples. There

were also my older cousins, Wade, Dale Davis, Walter Watt, and a special thanks to my big cousin, Kenneth Totten. This is the core group of men I sought out for good counsel.

## Proverbs 19:20-21

> Hear counsel, and receive instruction, that thou mayest be wise in thy latter end. 21 There are many devices in a man's heart; nevertheless the counsel of the LORD, that shall stand

MARSHON PEOPLES

# BULLET TWELVE

# EPIPHANY

My mother "is" a very talented, strong, high-spirited, no-nonsense kind of woman who loves to laugh and wants the best for me. She wasn't always able to give me what I wanted but always provided what I needed. As I said before, she raised me alone in our household. She worked for Washtenaw County throughout her life since 1978. From the Washtenaw County Parks and Recreation 4H to The Washtenaw County Sheriff's office to WCHO on Towner. She's worked all over the Washtenaw County area.

After we moved from Adams Street to Camelot Apartments on Washtenaw Avenue, I grew up as a "latchkey kid." What that means is, I had a key around my neck in school, which meant, "Come straight home after you get off the school bus, lock the door, and do not go outside unless I tell you to or until I'm at home. Do not touch the stove unless I tell you to. Do not let no one in the apartment unless I tell you to, and if you break any of these rules, you will get a punishment, and a backside reminder. Is that understood?" Lol. She also would not let me watch cartoons before or after school. Not until homework was done. Period with a 't' on it! Lol!

I had to grow up and figure out a lot of things on my own. Well, not alone; I had my God—who my mom said was my Heavenly Father—and trusted men at our church. But whenever something happened to me, my mother would say, "Go tell your Heavenly Father." She would often send me to go pray about matters, questions, or concerns I had. She would say, "God knows more than me. Go ask Him." And I would do just that. I would go to my room as before, remembering Elder Ross famously saying, "Did you pray?" And kneeling down to talk to my Heavenly Father like He was sitting in front of me. I mean, since they told me in church that God is everywhere, then I figured He was in my room, sitting in front of me too!

At a young age, I saw my mother's strength to make ends meet. She would come home tired, take her shoes off, and lay back in her chair with her eyes closed. Later it became customary for me to prepare a cold towel for her forehead and hot water on the stove for tea. She taught me to cook meals for us as she rested. Oftentimes, I would ask her to make a certain meal and she would usually say "It's food in the refrigerator. Go in there and make it yourself." And then I would go in the refrigerator and ask a bunch of questions on how to make it, whether it was fried chicken,

EPIPHANY

spaghetti, fried fish, tacos, hamburgers. It didn't matter; I would ask her how you make it. And she would say, while laying in the living room, "Go grab a skillet, put a little oil in it, turn the stove eye on medium heat…" and so we'd start my cooking lessons.

After a while, I stopped asking. I would go from house to house with my aunts—Felis, Sherita, and Renee—my cousins, and different people from the church. They all seemed to cook that good-tasting food! From Aunt Dot (Dorothy Watt) to Aunt Bert (Bert Totten); from Maretta Smith to Marsha Lathion (my mom's best friends); and Mother Grantham to Louis. And you can't forget Tommy Grantham. He made everything taste good! (Generations Bistro Soul Food (313) 305-4559). ~ Blessings

This is how I grew up, tasting LOVE in really good food. I'd wonder, "What's in this? What do I taste?" and try to make it at home. I even did it at restaurants. As I was learning to cook, I would ask my mom the measurements. "How much do I put in here?" She would always reply just like my grandma, and my great grandma would. "Put enough." Well, how much is enough? I learned to put enough in to make the food taste good to you! So that's what I kept doing. My mom would often taste my food and not say anything. I would be wondering and waiting for her to tell me if it was good or bad, but when she didn't say anything, it just meant that my food was good. If it was very good, she was like, "You got it from your mama!" We'd laugh!

I mention food often because it's how we showed LOVE. Fellowship, breaking bread, coming in, and supping with me, means more than just eating food. It is a way to bond and get fed emotionally, mentally, spiritually, *and* physically.

"Come and rest yourself" is what it all means. Some would call this a type of Communion or "foot washing," which represents inviting your brother "into" you as a brotherhood in your home.

In the Bible, when someone visited your home, you washed their feet because people wore sandals. Their feet would be dirty and tired from their journey. It was your privilege to invite your brother in to "sup" with you, for him to be refreshed or restored by washing his feet and feeding him.

EPIPHANY

Thereby, the accepted guest would honor the house of the one who washed their feet by breaking bread with their host, just as YAHuSHAuAH, i.e., Jesus washes us with His glory—His Blood, His Perfect Sacrifice—and feeds us His Living Bread—the Word of God in His Kingdom of Peace at HIS Table.

This was done once a year at Messias Temple, and I was honored to get to wash Elder Jesse Ross' feet. I can still hear him singing with his very deep and strong voice, *I Know It Was the Blood*. Welcome into the Sonship.

"Elder Peoples! Stand up. You are NOT to allow the towel you wash your brother's feet with to touch the ground. We must rewrap you with a fresh towel and start over washing your brother's feet."
~ Bishop Norman L. Wagner in Youngstown, Ohio

This also made me want to help my mom by earning my own money. I wanted nice clothes like the other kids, but I knew she couldn't always afford them. She would say, "Money don't grow on trees!" So, I would sell Kool-Aid (pronounced Koo - Laid, lol) in little bags for a quarter. The corners of my plastic sandwich bags for my school lunch would be missing from me ripping the corners, needing something to put my Kool-Aid in. This made my mom mad at first but then she laughed when she found out why the corners were missing. Her little boy wanted to help his Momma. Lol!

Later, in the seventh grade, I got that paper route I spoke of earlier. This paper route paid me $77 per week. One of my friends wanted to earn money too. So I paid him $25 per week to do my route. Then I went and got another route for myself. Well, more friends wanted to make money. So I ended up with five paper routes and didn't have to deliver a paper any more. I was a legitimate businessman earning $385 per week at the age of 12!

I bought my first real tie-up tie with some of the money I was making, and my cousin, Kenneth Totten, taught me how to tie it. I still admire him. Thanks, cuz! My family, mostly my Granddad, taught me hard work. But thanks to the "work smarter, not harder" pattern I learned from Elder Grayson, I continued to find ways to make money—from cutting hair to cutting grass, to drawing pictures for people, to designing murals in churches and homes. I was definitely

bitten by the entrepreneurial bug, and it's still that way to this day. I can help you too…
(visit www.The46thChamber.com)

My "Maker of Memories" M.O.M.
(Sunrise June 10, 1953 - Sunset January 18, 2020)
Rest in peace, Love

MARSHON PEOPLES

# BULLET THIRTEEN

# EPIPHANY

Over the years, my Mom and I would talk about almost anything, watch movies together, and laugh. She always took the time to correct me when I did something displeasing to her. She was strict, so that meant almost anything… lol!

I remember one time I had just gotten myself a used huffy bike! Oh, I loved that bike. It was a blue and white huffy bike from my neighborhood friend, Victor. I bought it for $25 with some of the money I got from watching after some younger boys from our church—Russell and Lamar. I used my bike to start my paper route with it. I would decorate my bike with a number plate, reflectors... you name it! New hand grips, pedals, and a laid-back seat post. Oh, you couldn't tell me that my bike wasn't one of the best in the Camelot apartment complex!

One day all my friends were going across this really busy street in the Ypsilanti and Ann Arbor area called Washtenaw. Now, my mother gave me a strict rule not to cross Washtenaw. I can play anywhere in the apartment complex and International Apartments, but I could not cross Washtenaw.

However, across Washtenaw was a restaurant called Arby's, and behind Arby's was this dirt bike ramp that we made that allowed us to jump high in the air. We could do table tops and tricks of all kinds. We called it "Arby's ramp." Well, as kids do, we thought we'd go have this fun and that our parents wouldn't find out. So I go across this busy street, looking both ways, being very careful, and I'm having fun with my friends jumping at Arby's ramp. We're doing tricks and tabletops. We're spinning in the air, trying to outdo one another in acrobatic moves with our bikes.

I get home, thinking she is not the wiser. A few days later, all of a sudden, I come home and my mother says "Go get your bike." "Why?!" I asked. "What's wrong?" With me thinking about getting my bike, I realized, "Uuuggghhh, she KNOWS!!!" She would give that stern scowl—the motherly look of disappointment. She had a way of poking out her lips in disgust, with her hands on her hips, to let me know she was truly displeased. She didn't have to say a word. I knew that she knew I crossed Washtenaw.

With her twisted, angry face, she said, "Now go get your bike out of your room.... take it... put it in the trash!!!!" I thought she might possibly be joking to teach me a lesson.

But she said, "I am not playing!" She made me grab my bike, she walked me outside, and watched me take the bike to the big garbage dumpster. I thought if I just put it by the dumpster it would be okay... NOT, lol. She said, "No, I said put it IN the trash." Furthermore, that year I got the chicken pox. One day we were at Elder and Mother Ross' house when I said, "I got bumps on me," and Sister Ross asked, "Does it look like it got water in them?" and I said "Yes." So she made this tea made with onions and (I think) garlic. I'm not certain what else was in it, but she had me drinking all the way down, and it brought the chicken pox all the way out the next day.

My mother called the Ypsilanti Press to tell them that I wouldn't be able to deliver the papers for a while. She didn't know about my paper route operation, and she came into my room and asked me, "Shon, how are your papers getting delivered?" With me not understanding that the Ypsilanti Press Newspaper was on the phone, I told my mother about my five friends who were helping me deliver my paper route, so they gave my routes to each of the five individual boys. Lol!

Here's a little word of advice to any young people who may be reading this book: Obey your parents. "Children, obey your parents in all things: for this is well pleasing unto the Lord." ~ Colossians 3:20

My mother and I would talk about the Word of God quite often. She would see something, and I would see something else. We would then discuss, agree, disagree, and, more often than not, see amazing revelations of God together. She focused more on the "speak to it" power of the Word. I was more fascinated with the mysteries of the "bloodline promises" power of the Word. Both are needed in understanding who you are in the Most High, Great I AM.

I grew to love God's Word more and more. I used to fall asleep trying to read the "thee's" and "thou's" of the passages. There was no Google at this time. I had to use a concordance, dictionary, Bible dictionary, KJV, Amplified, Scofield, and a 4-translation Thompson Chain Bible. Later I got into Hebrew and Aramaic Bibles.

Early in my childhood, my mother bought me Disney and Serendipity books since I loved to draw, but she really got them to help me read better—so I could comprehend what I was reading. One evening, she had me read this Disney Duck Tales book to her. She had the biggest laugh while I was reading about Huey, Dewey, and Louie because I couldn't say Huey; I kept saying Hooey! She turned so red from laughing. She said she thought it was so cute. Lol!

She was big on my reading and writing. She would make me write all my upper- and lower-case letters in cursive before I could go outside and play. She later bought me comic books, so when God would give me understanding, He would reveal His Word to me like the comics. This made me read the Bible like a comic book too! The Bible stories have giants, angels, warriors, kings, prophecies, and miracles. But more importantly, the Bible has promises and mysteries as well. I would read in pure wonderment and wanted to see these miracles in person. Not understanding at the time that I was living the miracles already.

Well, without a bike, I couldn't hang out with a lot of the kids in my apartment complex while they went riding. And with no paper route, I no longer had a newspaper delivery business. So I would walk all the way to Maplewood Apartments to hang out with Damond Mannon and Jack Lyons.

Cronemisis: Drawn and created by MarShon Peoples, 1988 (eighth grade)

# EPIPHANY

Jack was just always playing around and laughing, but he could have been a track star. Yes, he could really run! Real talk. Damond always wanted to listen to Run DMC. "Whose house? Run's house," and The Fresh Prince *Rock the House*. Also, going to hoop was a guarantee, so we would go to Eastern University's IM Rec building and the Bowen Field House. We would hoop until somebody kicked us out! Lol!

Damond was a left-handed phenom, and he was cooking a lot of the college kids! So obviously, I got better too. Plus, this was around the time I was hanging out with the Granthams, too, after church and on weekends. That left-handed Damond would burn me. Lol! So I had to stick him, forcing him right. And I had to jump backward, to put him back in front of me if he rocked me left for a fake or did a quick burst toward the rim. Sometimes he would do this move to spin back right! Either way, he was going to burn me and laugh at me. Needless to say, my defense got a workout everyday dealing with Damond Mannon. Thank you. (R.I.P. Bro! #WhenWeRockTheHouse)

However, at the age of 17, many temptations piqued my curiosity as well. I was approached countless times to sell drugs for various people. These young, wannabe gangsters would flash their cash, wear the apparel I wanted, and had cars, clout, and status.

I remember a time when I was just standing outside. A dark-gray car with big, shiny, silver rims pulled up. The man inside the car said, "Hey lil' dude! You want some Jordans?" I stood there and asked, "What do you mean?" The man said, "Look, all you need to do is take this package up to that door, and I will give you $100 to get some Jordans." He then took a $100 dollar bill and put it on top of the package, extending it out to me. "Look," he said, "just take this money and this package to that door, take what they give you, and bring what they give you back to me. I'll pay you another $100 for what you hand me."

I stood there a while, but just as I was about to take the man up on his offer, another teenager was walking past, and the man gave him the same offer. The young man took the package and money, did what the man said, returned, and handed the man an envelope. The man handed the young man another $100 and left. This transaction happened

EPIPHANY

within 30 seconds, right in front of me. All I could think of that day was, "In 30 seconds, a young man made $200!"

This began to really eat at me. My mind was in a whirlwind of lusting thoughts on how to make that kind of money. So much so that I began hanging with bad company. Thank God for the twins, Terry and Tracy, and big bro, Tyrone Williams for helping me stay out of trouble at the time. Thank you.

MARSHON PEOPLES

# BULLET FOURTEEN

# EPIPHANY

This one time, I was with some guys I had no business hanging out with. We were all up and around Detroit all night. The whole evening everyone was calling me by the name "Shon." When we arrived at another location, a mutual associate of ours looked in the car and said to me, "What up, MarShon!" Just then, one of the guys I had been with all evening turned and said, "MarShon?... MarShon Peoples?" Keep in mind, all evening, the guys were calling me "Shon." "Yeah?" I said to this guy who was questioning my name as we were all exiting the car.

As I think back, I should've known better that something was about to happen, especially with the kind of company I was with. Everything seemed to be in slow motion, like a movie. Except I wasn't watching; I was *in* this film sequence.

Immediately, this guy pulled out the biggest handgun ever and put it in my mouth. He had me on my back, laying on the hood of the car with my face facing upward. He began to question very sharply with strong force, asking if I knew a certain young lady. I said nothing but, unfortunately, yes, I knew her. I knew the certain referred-to young lady in a way that is intimate for a young man to know a young lady.

I began to think of all my loved ones at home and church. Tears began to stream as gravity pulled them to my ears, since I was laying on my back on the hood of the car. I thought I was done for sure. Just then, our mutual associate had his gun pointed at the head of the one who held me captive, saying to my current nemesis, "Let my boy up! You don't check my boy. You need to check your girl... She cheated on you, he didn't. Now let him up." My current assailant pulled the gun out of my mouth, wiped my tears with his own sleeve, and put the safety of the gun on... "Click!"

That click sound... It did something to me. All my fear and anger consumed me. In other words, some would say I "snapped." With one motion, I snatched his gun from his hand... As a number of people pulled me off the guy, I stood shivering in pure fear, thinking, I will never hang with this crowd again." And I didn't. I figured I was better off sticking with my church friends, but this didn't stop Satan's continued attempts to destroy me.

EPIPHANY

## Psalm 27:5

> For in the time of trouble he shall hide me in his pavilion: in the secret of his tabernacle shall he hide me; he shall set me up upon a rock

Flash forward to, January 6, 2012: *I hear a BOOM! Then... darkness... I can't see. I can't move. I feel like I'm floating. I can't hear anything... Oh! There's a sound... faint pop-like sound in the distance... Are they still shooting? Lord, not like this... not like this... Is this it? Is this how I'm about to go?...*

Another evening comes to mind, as my true friends from church and I all piled into one car to go to Detroit for the African Festival at Hart Plaza. This was good, clean fun with friends. The company I was with was great, the food was to die for, and the afro-centric culture was awesome. However, on the car ride home, the car broke down on the wrong side of Detroit.

We had to park the car by the overpass and walk to the gas station to use the payphone. It was hot that day, but cold that night. We finally reached the gas station. Cold and tired, I sat down to rest on the cinder block foundation of the gas station's marquis sign.

That night it was Mark, Darrin, Robert, Ryan, and myself. Mark was on the phone, attempting to call a relative to see if we could lodge with them for the evening. All of a sudden, this car at the gas pump speeds off with the pump still connected to the car's gas tank. I remember thinking, "Only in the D." Well, from that point on, I'm in prayer with my God saying, "Lord, you gotta get me home."

Just then, this man approaches me. I was still seated on the cinder block foundation when I looked up at him as if to say, "Man, what do you want?" But me and the guy didn't exchange words. He simply walked away. Afterward, I turned to look at my friends, and they were gone, except for Mark, who was still on the pay phone. When Mark ends his phone conversation, he turns and says to me, "Where did everybody go?!" "I don't know!" I reply, "I was sitting right here." Mark then asks a rhetorical question: "Why would they leave us alone on the bad side of Detroit?!"

EPIPHANY

Our friends left us, but God didn't. Mark and I were furious when we looked down the street, across the bridge, to see our comrades at such a distance. When we finally rejoined each other, both parties were yelling at one another.

Mark and I were yelling at them for leaving, but the others were yelling about something much more troubling. My best friend Robert got my attention and said, "Shon!!!! We were screaming at the top of our lungs to run! He got a gun!!! He got a gun!!!! The man who walked up to you had a gun!!! You just sat there!!! He had it pointed at your head!!!

## Psalm 23:4

> Yea, though I walk through the valley of the shadow of death, I will fear no evil: for thou art with me; thy rod and thy staff they comfort me

You didn't see it?!!!" No, I didn't see a gun. I was in prayer: "Lord you gotta get me home." Just like when the young man had the gun in my mouth, once again, my "head" was under attack.

The Bible says, "Let this mind be in you, which was also in Christ Jesus." If my mind is destroyed, then I cannot fulfill His purpose. We settled at this party store. I listened as they all gave their perspectives on what had just happened. We tried calling and hailing cabs, but none of them would stop.

Mark finally had to call his brother-in-law back in Ypsilanti to come get us. As we waited, this unseemly man walked up and said, "Ya'll alright?" We all replied that we were good. He then goes on to say, "If ya'll need to use the phone, my brother stays right across the street." We all replied with gratitude. But one by one, more men just like the one who was speaking to us, began to surround us. We started devising a plan to run in a certain direction, because we didn't know what these men were about to do, and we wasn't sticking around to find out.

We were in that "on the count of 3" mode. Just then, a police officer shows up and says, "Where's the party?!" I reply, "No party!" But my friends and I rush to the officer's car. We tell him our situation. The officer made the crowd disperse and promised to continue to check on us until our ride showed up.

Well, the good thing is, Mark's brother-in-law showed up. The funny thing is, he showed up in a Corsica with his wife and two kids in the car. So, five sizable teenage boys had to fit in the back seat. It was tight but right, and that night God covered me yet again, and got me home.

The next day was Sunday. We all sang in the choir. Mark stands up and gives his testimony of what happened the night before, mentioning the tragedy that was almost me. One by one, each of my brothers in the Lord stood and told the magnificence of God concerning me. How the man had a gun to my head, but I did not move. I was the only one left. The whole church looked at me in silence and when I stood I just shook my head, then said, "I didn't see a gun," and the congregation blew up into a thunderous praise to our God.

MARSHON PEOPLES

# BULLET FIFTEEN

# EPIPHANY

This was a very trying time for me. On one side, I am receiving some of the most powerful knowledge of God known to man: highly respected at church, singing in the youth choir; and on the other side, I'm constantly at odds with my mother, not liking myself, and perpetually in trouble, getting into fights in high school and the local area. I didn't start fights, but like David, I definitely tried to finish them. I wasn't allowing anyone to bully me. I was literally at a crossroads.

Ironically, God was calling me to the ministry at this time. At 17 years old, I don't answer the call. Instead, I focused on trying to just be a "good Christian" by keeping to myself at home and studying the Word of God. Not knowing I was preparing for the inevitable... My anointing.

High school was very confusing. Not because of the school work; it was the distractions. Trying to do the school work and trying to learn what the teacher really wanted you to know beyond all the games that it seemed like the teachers tried to play to make sure you couldn't learn, like piling on tons of homework that had to be done the very next day. At least, that's how I felt at the time.

I was playing football, too, so practice was on top of all that. But enjoying myself during the summer football practice! We had three-a-day practices: weight training, conditioning, special teams, and our famous "Brave Drills." I remember when I first put on the helmet and shoulder pads with the whole uniform on. It did something to me. I wanted to play running back, but we had a runner who was a much stronger runner than I was. His name is K. Mayes. He had very Barry Sanders-like qualities in his running style. I knew that I was going to have my work cut out for me.

One day I went down to "the valley," as I called it, behind Putt Putt on Eastlawn to visit my friend DeVaughn (yes, the same one). There was Robert Addie and a bunch of people from the Southside hanging out at his house in the garage. "Are you playing football?" they asked me. "Yeah," I said. They asked me what position. I said, "Running back," and they all laughed. "You ain't going to get tick because Ken is going to have all that time!" And all of that time, he did get haha! But I got a few snaps.

## EPIPHANY

I remember during one game, Coach put me in to run the 38. That's when you run to the sideline, spreading out the defense as far as you can so the team can set up the next play for either a run up the middle, or pass down the other side of the field. But this particular day, I wanted to try do something other than just spread the defense. I was going to go for it! I ran the 38 to the edge of my line, then cut to run up the field.

A linebacker met me right there at the shoulder. I cut back to head for the outside. I staggered like I was about to go out of bounds. I then tried cut to get back in again. He was right there with me again. I had no other place to go, but to the outside all the way, real hard, and try to curl that edge on it. And I got it! He ran alongside me, matching me, speed for speed. I didn't have any blockers out there over on that side

of the visitor's side of the field. I was hoping I could get that touchdown, but I got the first down! As I got it, he hit me in such a way to try to draw the ball loose. When I finally hit the ground, he tried to sneak in and pop it out of my hand at the same time, but I held on.

The referee blew the whistle, and he came and grabbed the ball. "You're alright, you are alright, good job!" I was surprised that he said it, but when I looked at the scene where I was on the field, I had gotten the first down and more!

In another game, we were playing away at Tecumseh High School. Coach Nedella put me in at the very end of the game. He asked me, "Did you get in yet?" I said, "No." He put me in for the last play of the game. I saw this player—number 47 linebacker—and we ran my play 38 once again. I yelled out, "I see you, 47!" He was on the opposite side of the field. "47 you're mine, 47 you're mine!" I didn't play the majority of that game because Ken was the starter (for one), I had twisted my ankle in gym class (for two), and it was a challenging game (for three).

We were down a touchdown and a field goal. But I wanted to play. I taunted him to come at me, and I ran at him as soon as the ball was hiked. I turned to go towards my quarterback, got the handoff, and the whole line shifted to the opposite side where I was positioned prior to the snap. It was a clear, open field. The only thing between me and that touchdown was a safety.

# EPIPHANY

At that point, I bore down. I reared at him, running straight at him like I was going to run him over, and at the last second, I cut, and cut again. Thanks, Smitty. I got that from you! Lol.

Kept running... kept running... and all of a sudden, my foot hit this dip in the grass. "Oh no, I hurt my ankle again!" I tried my best to continue to run to get the touchdown, but the other team caught me from behind. I still pulled forward, thinking I was still setting my team up for a nice touchdown. When I got to about the five-yard line, the game was over. There was no more opportunity for my team to get in that touchdown to score. I sat there in the grass with a hurt ankle and watched as my team walked toward the bus.

I gathered myself and said, "Lord, thank you for the opportunity." I wanted another shot. I listened to my coaches, I watched how different people played, and I watched as my friends excelled on the field at school. Some of my teammates I played with, I felt I was just as "good (as them) in the hood," but when I got to school it was a much different ball game.

We had fun in the hood! Me, Rob "G" and a few others. We'd play a good game in a field somewhere, having a good old time. But at school, all bets were off. It was every man for himself. I learned that late (and the hard way) later in high school. I figured I was better on defense at Free Safety because I could read the offense better. (I used to be the backup running back). I could see what they were about to do before they did it. Plus, I had been watching the High School Safety phenom. No need for introduction in Ypsi; we call him "Cheese" (R.I.P. Thank you. #Brave 4ever).

I can respect my teammates for different reasons, and it really had nothing to do with football; most of it had to do with their leadership skills. Like Kip Johnson (currently co-owner of Blackstone Bookstore and Culture Center with Carlos Franklin)—how hard he went in practice. Rob G Addie (owner of blessedbrimz.org caps)—he has a slender build, but he will push up the weights of the heaviest of stacking! DeVaughn was very smart! No, like 4.0 GPA smart! He was an architect at stealing bases in baseball too. He and Kip started weaving in between the tackles, making people miss. When Marvin Wilson (rest in peace bro ✊)

caught the ball as our #1 receiver, #3 in the State, you wasn't catching him with the ball in hand in the open field! He himself, with his long strides. And his tall body would cause him to beat defenders. All Derrell Brooks or Chris Tice had to do was just launch it in his direction, and he was most likely going to catch it.

That was the fun part of high school, but my body was going through changes, as most teenagers do. The Bible teachers are saying one thing, and my body is saying another. I'm asking questions about the changes, and all the older men seemed to do was give me a smirk and say, "You will be alright." Lol! But I wanted answers. I wanted to know why my body was doing the things it was doing, regardless of thought content or people around. The body does what it needs to do to grow—to transform into manhood.

YOUNG MEN: Proper hygiene is a MUST! If you have an asthma inhaler, I pray for your healing. But the asthma inhaler medicine gets down into your esophagus and the medicine can sour your throat. So gargle with baking soda, dilute some apple cider vinegar with some water, and drink it. This will help with your esophagus and freshen your throat and breath. (Alcoholic mouthwash makes it worse). My friends were going through their drama, too, with the ups and downs of their teenage years. Not a kid, but not an adult. From us hearing our parents say, "You know better than that!" To, "You think you grown; you ain't grown!"

This one time I'm chillin' by myself in an empty classroom that Elder Lundy taught us in at our church. Bo happened to see me and came into the classroom too. "What's wrong with you?" As he noticed my posture. I replied, "Man, my moms just be mad at me... I try to stay out of the way." His response let me know that he understood what I was going through. "Man, my dad is acting the same way! I don't get it!"

We're sitting there understanding each other's situation in a serious yet funny moment, like two blues brothers about to go in on a harmonica tune. One minute, we're on top of the world, with everyone proud of us—completing our major milestone of high school. And the next minute, reality hit us. After high school, you're just another body in the house. Time to make some decisions.

# EPIPHANY

Time to step into manhood. As I said before, Brad Holman would come get me and my church fellas so we could hoop. This gave me a lot of comfort at the time. Going to hoop got me out of the house. I got to hang out with friends.

There was James Rush, the Ebony Assassin. His inside outside game was Jordanesque. Can turn it on to win, but if he doesn't have to, he ain't gonna. At least until someone makes him mad. Then it's serious. Lol!

Robert "Bo-Nice" Lucas. His favorite player is Magic, so Bo would back you in and use that body with the baby ski hook. You can't stop it. He'll dot your eye from the 3 outside too! Then there was Henry "Slim" aka H-Town Frost, the high flier who could easily hit his head on the rim!

Sometimes Danny "Daniel Son" Tardy was there. He was the "X Factor"—the dude who hits quiet shots from deep. Of course, Brad "The Professor" Holman, the Mastermind behind us coming together. He really showed us how to play basketball, not hoop. We knew how to hoop from the hood, but basketball was something different. Then there was me—"The Watchman." Not like that, lol! Brad would have me bring the ball up and see it all unfold.

And usually, he had me stick with the fastest player on defense. "Look at what you got!" That's what he would say to me every time I came up the court, "Look at what you got!" With those words, I could zone out……. from problems…… on the hoop court…….. with my brothers in Christ. Oh! I loved to "pick pockets" or what I like to say, "Got 'em!" Basically, steal the basketball, aka "the Rock." Then drive to the hole and/or roll a dime.

I had fun hooping with Brad. He had sayings like, "Look at what you got!", "Run it, Shon!" and "Too easy!" It would make people miss the easiest of shots… lol! Another is my favorite. It wasn't an instruction toward us boys; it was more like a sound he would make before he burned an opponent... and burn them he would. The sound was somewhat like a quick juke move sound of "gotcha." The noise was a "Augh!!!" Lol, my friends and church mates know what I'm saying. He played kinda like Vinnie Johnson —strong, broad, and knows how to use his leverage.

We would go from court to court hooping all day on a Saturday. I could be at peace on the court. While others took our games seriously, some of my friends would even get mad because I would be laughing while playing ball. I wanted to win for sure, and usually we did with some epic runs, but hoop was fun for me. A hoop court is a true battlefield. However, it was a battlefield I enjoyed. No worries, problems, or blame. Just the ball, the court, and my brothers in the Lord. It was the best place for me to be.

In later years, we even won a first-place trophy together in 1997 at a Church Basketball tournament hosted by Burning Bush's pastor, Bishop Don Shelby, at Ypsilanti High School. We contested some of the local churches and a few from the Metro Detroit area. These churches all had ballers. It was a battle for us at Messias Temple Church from the start because we lost our first game, which put us in the lower bracket, and we had to literally climb our way back to the final game.

We had a very nice squad, but we were missing our very best—the late superstar wide receiver and my high school football teammate, Marvin Wilson, and his ballin' brother, Jimmy "JDub" Wilson. I was focusing on a church named Shiloh because I think to this day the whole church can hoop! Lol! Plus, Shiloh had an Ypsilanti High School school phenom from back in the day on their family church team, in the person of number Big 50 Shannon "Bam!" Aka "We wanna BAM dunk" Williams, on their talented squad.

As we're running our gauntlet of back to back to back games to climb out of the lower bracket, teams are dwindling. The gym is becoming quieter as the crowd fades with each eliminated team. I felt good… like we can win this! Everyone on our team is clicking, "the flow" was definitely on with Brad at the helm. However, someone different from our team always stepped up each game and had a "shine" moment game. Whoever was knocking them down, we just kept feeding the one with the hot hand.

There was a game we (well… at least I) thought would be our final game, but surprisingly, it was not: our game against Shiloh—this church from Detroit who had a tough team with an even tougher pastor. This was an extremely high-spirited, very physical game. You know, "Ghetto Ball" hard fouls and all. But we from the hood too, so… we won! "Not so fast! said the pastor from the D with this loud, harsh, stern, bishop-like tone…

EPIPHANY

We were undefeated, and they lost a game! And he went on to say, "Isn't this a two-game elimination tournament?!" My thoughts were that the championship game was a sudden-death game—winner takes all. But the boisterous pastor continued, "I bet if we played with fouls called, we'd win!" In my book, they brought the physical, so we played the physical, and both sides were making contact. I was so very tired. Plus, you know how when you've been ballin' all day, and your toes start pushing against the front of your shoes so that they hurt. Lol!

Well, I kept standing because I knew if I sat down, my feet would be done. I had given my all to the game I thought was the final, and still the pastor continued. So much so Brad, our mentor, turned to us and asked, "Well what y'all wanna do?" We all looked at each other and I took my towel and spun it above my head like a helicopter with a shout "Possess the land! Possess the land!" My church teammates joined in the shout with me and started laughing, then said, "Alright." At this point I was exhausted, so I sat out (my feet were pulsating and I had to keep standing) at least for the first quarter to give myself a chance to muster up another wind to help in any way I could to help us win.

However, none of us on the side had to. We had a ram in that Burning Bush's Church Basketball tournament in the person of Danny Tardy. I know some people reading, especially our friends, might be laughing, but Daniel Son balled out with the 3-point ball!! No, seriously he can play. He makes you laugh and he's an MJ fanatic... I mean both of MJ's!! Michael Jordan and Michael Jackson. Lol!

The game frustrated the team from "the D" (that's what we call Detroit) so bad that the center on the other team slammed my boy—the high flier of our team, Henry Frost III—to the court hard. Pastor Shelby then called the game. "Game over. Messias Temple Church are the victors!" Each of us were rewarded with these beautiful "iced" trophies. Pastor Shelby definitely has taste.

Our pastor Bishop Harry S. Grayson acknowledged us at church the next day. We had all brought our trophies with us, but we didn't hold them up. It wasn't about the trophy; it was about our triumph together. I still have it to this day.

"Together we can do it"
The late great Melvin "Bible Walker" Bass

MARSHON PEOPLES

# BULLET SIXTEEN

# EPIPHANY

Many wonder why I am so passionate about ministering to high-risk youth. My response is always the same: "Because they are me at that age." I was confused, scared, and lacked direction. I thought I knew best, but I didn't know me because I was not allowing the Holy Ghost to guide me. Thank God He was and is still with me, despite myself. Looking back, I realize this was exactly 20 years before I meet the designated bullet I call Epiphany.

So then, something pivotal happened to launch me into my next level of anointing. Just like when David killed the lion and the bear: 30-fold anointing. Then he killed Goliath: 60-fold anointing. And when he became king: 100-fold anointing. So I'm ready, Lord. Anoint me again.

"Anointed simply means to be chosen formally by God to do a specific task or many tasks."
   ~ Bishop Norman L. Wagner

In 1993, I was hanging out at the University of Michigan (U of M) with my best friend, Robert Lucas. He was a student there, but I attended Washtenaw Community College. For the time being, that is.

You see, while hanging out we were at the Art and Architecture building, located on the north campus in Ann Arbor at U of M.

We were just drawing and having fun when a professor walked past and said, "I just love U of M students!" I replied, "I'm sorry, sir, but I don't go here." The professor looked at my artwork and asked, "Would you like to attend here?" "Yeah!" I replied. The professor then introduced me to the Dean of the Art School—Dr. Jean Pijanowski.

Dr. Pijanowski was a kind, high-spirited, and easy-to-talk-to kind of guy. I sat down in his office, and he said, "Let's take a look, since you come recommended." He took one look at my artwork and said, "You want to come here?" "Yes!" I said. "Great!" he replied. "Have you applied to the University of Michigan?" I replied again, "Yes, but a Rhonda Gilmore won't accept me." Dr. Pijanowski then picked up the phone and called Undergraduate Admissions at U of M. "Yeah, Rhonda?" he said. "It's Jean! Listen, you have a kid on your register by the name of MarShon Peoples?" Her response had to be "yes" based on his next words: "Great! Accept him!" Then he hung up the phone!

EPIPHANY

I was happy and stunned as he stretched forth his hand, saying, "Welcome to University of Michigan! Is there anything else?!" With a prestigious, jolly grin on his face. Still amazed, I responded, "My mom can't afford this school." Dr. Pijanowski had a quick rebuttal: "You have a scholarship! Is there anything else?" Dumbfounded I said, "I guess not." And with another confirming handshake, he said again, "Welcome to the University of Michigan." God used my gift of drawing to show Himself strong for me to attend a top-notch, prestigious university and showed Himself to be a provider constantly throughout the duration of my attendance at the University of Michigan.

U of M was like a whole new world. New people and backgrounds. I saw many strange things attending the university, in that I was exposed to many diverse cultures, ideals, religions, and methods. None of these people I encountered were ashamed to outwardly express their ethos (ways of thinking). Regardless of our differences, I developed a level of respect for them, due to them being true to their "truths."

I began to compare the many words I would hear in messages from some preachers, pastors, and teachers, with their actions. Although, while orating their messages, they were very profound, their lives didn't seem to reflect their own words. In other words, "not being true to their truths." As the scripture says, "Having a form of godliness, but denying the power thereof: from such turn away" (2 Timothy 3:5). So, I wanted to know more about my God and what I was missing.

While attending U of M, I took a few history classes. One was Biblical Hebrew, so I could better understand the Old Testament, and the other was the History of the Holy Bible. This was way different from learning in church. These classes taught me things that I wasn't previously taught. My instructor at the University of Michigan went in depth about the holy wars, Constantine Edicts, Arians, Spanish Inquisition, conquistadors, and more. The only familiar topic to me was "The Council of Nicaea," which I learned about in church. College taught that there were more councils altogether!

EPIPHANY

My Hebrew class especially intrigued me. This was also around the time I was really listening to the late great Johnny James and Bishop Young as they expounded on the Name YHWH. This class taught me that each letter was a word, each word was a sentence, each sentence was a paragraph, every word had meaning, and every meaning had a thought that hinged upon something else that had to materialize when you spoke it.

For instance, the Name Yahweh or Jesus, which means "The Lord Saves"—spelled "yod hey waw hey" or "YHWH"—really holds a much more meaningful definition than given in English. There are many dialects that cause scholars and theologians to argue about the Name. When, in fact, no matter what language you speak, it comes back to mean LIFE or, more personally said, "I AM."

I am giving a quick Hebrew lesson. The letter "Y" or "yod" in Hebrew means "hand." The letter "H" or "hey" means "behold." And the letter "W" or "waw" means "nail." Subsequently, in a sentence it would say, "Behold the hand behold the nail" in English. My mind immediately goes to the Cross where Jesus shed His blood and His breath/spirit. In other words, He gave His Life.

The meaning in Hebrew would be "I Am Almighty." YAH means I AM. AH means Almighty. Furthermore, The "YH" means the inhale, and "WH" is the exhale. Put it together, and you have breath or life.

Many places in the Bible where YHWH was, it was replaced with the words, "the LORD." "SHA" in Hebrew means "salvation" or "the action of the Word of God." This would read as YAHuSHAuAH (Joshua) meaning "deliverance" (I AM Salvation Almighty). Some may even say YAHuAHShi (I AM Almighty to My Salvation) or AHAWAYAHuSHI (Love I AM to My Salvation).

It was here I learned that we were speaking Hebrew in church every time we said "Hallelujah." We were told that it meant "the highest praise you can give the Lord," which is true. However, "Hallel" in Hebrew means "praise(s);" the "u" is a sound that means "to something;" and "yah" or "jah" means "I AM." So the word "Hallelujah" is really a sentence: "Hallelu Yah" or "Praise to The I AM." I AM so glad to have learned I AM His praises.

EPIPHANY

# BULLET
## SEVENTEEN

It was 1994 in Indianapolis, Indiana, at a PAW National Church Convention. I was 19 turning 20. My cousins, Dion, Harold, and I were trying to check into our hotel, but to our dismay, our reservation had already been given away to another customer, and the hotel was fully booked. We all came from different sides of the state and basically bummed rides from other saints to get to the convention in the first place.

We were literally all sitting on the curb with all our luggage. We sat trying to figure out what we were going to do. My cousin, Dion, attended Christ Temple in Muskegon Heights, where Diocesan Bishop Willie Burrel was pastor at the time. Many of my family members, including my grandparents, attended Christ Temple. So did we before we moved to Ypsilanti, as stated before. So my family was pretty close with the Burrels'. We called our good friend Joseph Burrel—the youngest of the bishop's 12 children—to see if his father had any extra rooms.

I had a close relationship with Bishop Burrel as well. Ever since I was very young, whenever I came to Muskegon to visit my grandparents, Bishop would see me at church and say, "My friend, Shon!" I would reply, "I missed you, Bishop!"

He would then say, "How many birthdays have I missed?" No matter what the number was, the bishop would reach into his pocket and give me about $10 or $20, then escort me to the fellowship hall of the church, where some of the most delicious breakfast would be served. And the biscuits! The biscuits had to be a descendant of God's manna! They were these homemade-from-scratch delights, oven-baked to a golden brown color, with a slight crisp on the edges. These delectable breakfast treats were often savored by themselves or with jelly and sausage. I want some right now!

Bishop Burrel would say, "This is my friend, Shon, and his breakfast is always *free* whenever he comes to town. Give him whatever he wants." I'd reply, "I love you, Bishop!" So, our hope was pretty high that the bishop would have an extra room for us. Joseph called us back, stating that Bishop had one more room left at the Omni and we could have it, with a message from Bishop to me, "Anything for my friend, Shon." My cousins and I were so relieved! We ran all the way to the Omni, since we didn't have a car and didn't have time to find a ride.

As we approached the front door of the hotel, some other guests were trying to use the luggage carrier but got stuck in the swivel door. So my cousins and I had to use the side door to enter. We finally got to the counter, and the desk clerk told us the reservation had been given away!

My cousin Dion began to talk to the clerk, informing her of the situation and what we just went through... but I began to pray. Just then, the clerk said, "We have one more room in the hotel, and since we gave your room to someone else, we have to give you the penthouse for the price of your original room." Talk about going from the gutter most to the uttermost!!!

We were elated, especially after we saw the room! A penthouse suite and it was huge!! I'm talking about two huge beds, double doors, kitchen, living room, a special key to get up to our floor, and a beautiful walkout rooftop view! It is in the bleakest situations our faith pleases God, and He surpasses our understanding.

# EPIPHANY

The next day, I was in line getting some food and telling of what God had done for my cousins and me. I began talking and referencing scriptures about Jesus. This Bishop happened to overhear me. I couldn't remember his name for the longest time. He said to me, "Young man, you are a minister." And I replied to the bishop, "Uh... no sir... I am not. I simply just love the Word of God."

He stepped closer to me, gave me a stern look with a grin, and said, "You are a minister; you just haven't answered the call." I went to speak again, and he held up his hand to silence me. He said, "Shhhh, your words carry too much weight to let them hit the ground." Then he simply walked away. That Bishop was none other than the late great Bishop Norman L. Wagner.

Bishop Norman L. Wagner
(January 14, 1942 – January 30, 2010)

That evening I went to one of the convention's church services. In the service I went to, Marvin Sapp happened to be preaching about "purpose." The service was super hype! I remember young people from far and wide praising and magnifying God. My friend, Marlon Reid, seemed to be leading the praise with his extreme worshiping style! I, on the other hand, was meditating on the word that had just been delivered. In my heart, I heard the call of the Lord to the ministry.

EPIPHANY

It seemed audible within me, saying, "Now, will you speak to my people...?" The next morning before checkout, we received a call from the front desk informing us that the repair for the swivel door would be $1000. I replied, "Do you know the people who broke the door?" The clerk responded, "We were told your room is responsible." I replied, "That simply is not true. We came through the side door. We are Christians, and if we had broken the door, we definitely would try to pay for it." The desk clerk responded, "We will be calling you, or this will be handled when you check out." The clerk abruptly hung up the phone.

I lay in bed, perplexed at this current dilemma. I then decided, "I'm gonna pray about this." I got out of bed, went to kneel down beside the bed, and before my knees could hit the floor, the thought dropped into my heart, "Get up." This shocked me into wonder. I questioned, "Is this you, Lord? Or is this just a thought in my head?" But, at the same time, I had this peace about the "swivel door dilemma."

My cousins, Dion and Harold, had awoken and questioned me about the phone call. As I revealed the nature of the call, Dion interrupted me and said, "We know we didn't break the door, and God will bring it to light." Sure enough, at checkout, the clerk said to us, "The door has been taken care of, and you are free to go." My God provides yet again for me.

## Psalm 91:1

> He that dwelleth in the secret place of the Most High shall abide under the shadow of the Almighty.

EPIPHANY

# BULLET EIGHTEEN

After I had returned home from the church convention in Indianapolis, I was cutting my hair when a scripture suddenly dropped into my mind: Ezekiel 2:4. This scripture just kept ringing in my head, like a splinter in my mind. So with my hair half cut on my head, I went to look up the scripture in the Bible to see what it says. It reads... "For they are impudent children and stiffhearted. I do send thee unto them; and thou shalt say unto them, Thus saith the Lord God."

I was in awe, disbelief, and denial. Recall of the church convention flooded and overflowed my memory with the words of the (at the time) "unknown Bishop" when I was standing in line getting food; the "purpose" message preached by Marvin Sapp; and God's provisions at The Omni Hotel—blessing my cousins and me, literally from street to penthouse.

I told myself, "Naw... Just a coincidence." Still refusing what I knew in my heart: God was calling me to the ministry. Within myself, I felt that same spiritual pull as I did at 6 years old—when God was calling me to salvation—to continue reading the Ezekiel passage etched in my thoughts. Ezekiel 2:5-8 goes on to say:

EPIPHANY

5 And they, whether they will hear, or whether they will forbear, (for they are a rebellious house,) yet shall know that there hath been a prophet among them.

6 And thou, son of man, be not afraid of them, neither be afraid of their words, though briers and thorns be with thee, and thou dost dwell among scorpions: be not afraid of their words, nor be dismayed at their looks, though they be a rebellious house.

7 And thou shalt speak my words unto them, whether they will hear, or whether they will forbear: for they are most rebellious.

8 But thou, son of man, hear what I say unto thee; Be not thou rebellious like that rebellious house: open thy mouth, and eat that I give thee.

As I sat there staring at the Bible, I still said to myself, "You're just thinking things." And "You're reading too far into it." Just then (I can say this now) the Lord immediately spoke to my heart, two more scriptures:

## Deuteronomy 18:18

I will raise them up a Prophet from among their brethren, like unto thee, and will put my words in his mouth; and he shall speak unto them all that I shall command him.

## Acts 3:22

For Moses truly said unto the fathers, A prophet shall the Lord your God raise up unto you of your brethren, like unto me; him shall ye hear in all things whatsoever he shall say unto you.

# EPIPHANY

After reading these scriptures and more, I dropped my Bible, jumped up, and ran upstairs to my mother, saying, "Mama, I've been called to the ministry!!" My mother calmly responded, "I already know. So has Janelle Toney (aka Janelle Phoenix Toney). Now go back downstairs and pray."

I marveled at my mother's words and demeanor as I went back downstairs in a daze, with my incomplete haircut. But I did as she instructed and, yet again, began to pray. After I got done with my prayer, my mom went on to say, "You and Janelle have to be processed for what you know and for what kind of anointing is in you both." She continued, "And you have to stay prayed up!"

In 18 years, I will meet the designated bullet I call Epiphany. Epiphany will lodge into and fracture my skull, pushing bone fragments closer to my brain, and tearing the outer membrane lining of my brain, with the bullet trapped in my brain—only a pocket of air between it and my brain…

"My brain is the quintessential piece of my body that makes me... me! My desires, secrets, fears, memories, dreams, and intellect inhabits... my mind with purpose. The body cannot live without the mind."

~ Morpheus, *The Matrix*, 1999

We all have a purpose, including Epiphany. At the age of 21, I answered the call to the ministry. "Hello? Yes, this is MarShon Peoples. The Ministry? Yes, I accept. But um... What do I do now? Do I just speak the Word of the Lord?"

EPIPHANY

# BULLET NINETEEN

My heart's desire was to sing! My aunt Sherita would sing to me when I was little, "Keep your mind stayed on Jesus, keep your mind stay on the Lord." ♪♪ Growing up, she also had the best gospel album collection in gospel music! Artists like: Dottie Peoples (no relation that I know of, but, skip it: "Hey Auntie!" lol), Andre Crouch, Walter Hawkins, Tremaine Hawkins, Rance Allen, The Clark Sisters, The Winans, and my favorite group, Commissioned.

I would visit my aunt and listen to her albums for hours and hours. The music would tell a story and make me feel free. Songs like, "I'm Going Away" and "I'm Going Up Yonder" would put me into a mindset that I could be somewhere without pain, fear, or death. A lot of the songs spoke of heaven like it hasn't yet happened, or is going to happen; but Commissioned songs were much different. They sang songs in a way that made it seem like heaven is "right now" for you and I. Songs like "My Secret Place," "I Am Here," and "Cry On" are all melodies that minister to me in my times of need.

EPIPHANY

Commissioned also had a way of singing that gave their songs layers upon layers of notes—harmonies and unison vocals playing with the sound of the horns, the bass, the organ, the drums, and the symbols. Their words would overlap one another and pause, and they would say faint words off in the distance—all nuggets of hidden treasures that you cherish as you listen to each and every single song.

What I love most of all about Commissioned is that they were singing the Word of God! I would listen closely and hear some of the songs matching some of the Holy scriptures that I had read in my previous days of study. I would run to tell my friends that they're singing this scripture or singing that scripture, and we would run to the Bible to look up the scriptures and read them and search the meanings as we listened to the Commissioned songs, over and over again.

We loved doing this so much that we started our own group called Dominion! Darrin Patterson (later sang background for Fred Hammond, Lexi, Rod Lumpkins, Mitchell Jones, and more), Kevin Toney (worshiper, songwriter, and nephew of Karl Reid from Commissioned),

Lance Bennett (songwriter), Loren Reeves and I were the singers. As for the instrumentalists, we had Chip Dixson (plays all instruments—drums being his first love—and has produced many songs since), Al Dumas on the organ and keys, and Henry Frost III on the drums (older brother to the Detroit psalmist, Tony Frost and son of Henry "Butch" Frost, the awesome left-handed bass player).

We were basically Commissioned wannabes, but our hearts were in the right place. Our songs, too, were laced with scripture and melodies and overlays since we listened to Commissioned so often. We emulated who sang what part. "I got Fred's part!" "I got Mitchell's part!" "I got Keith's part!" "I got Carl's part!" "I got Marvin's part!" and so on we went.

We would often go over to Chip's house to rehearse. His mother, Brenda Bird (Messias Temple choir director, vocal coach, and a great psalmist), was so gracious to let us make all that noise in her house all the time LOL. We would search from church to church, trying to find spots to rehearse so we could sing at different invites that we'd gotten.

# EPIPHANY

We all had our own strengths. Darrin was the one that made sure our melodies and harmonies were blended tight and sounded good. Chip and Al were the ones to make sure the music was on point. Chip was also the one to let us know when something was "nekkit" or "bott," i.e., if we or the music sounded bad. And "Pure D Hmmm Nekkit" if it was horrible. He was also quick to say "YeSir Docteeee" if the music was good LOL. I was the one that made sure we got together for rehearsals, and sometimes we had to just pile into my little 91 Ford Escort together! Lol

It didn't matter to me if we sounded good or bad to anyone else; as long as it sounded good to the Most High. I enjoyed the camaraderie, the singing, the coming together, the laughter, and the music. It was my escape, my way of telling a story in song. It was my way of being free, and whom the Son sets free is free indeed! To me, this was ministry: helping people feel better, helping them feel what you feel when a song is playing, and the music vibrating through the atmosphere, ushering in the presence of the Most High God.

Many people would try to tell me what "ministry" is and how to become a minister. The definition that was bestowed upon me by man was:

First, I had to be "faithful" by being at church every time the doors were open. I had to go to 52 bible classes to start—basically, a full year. This made my mother angry, given that I was raised in the church and the current pastor knew me intimately and had taught me over the years. We even had a videotape of me receiving the gift of the Holy Ghost.

Then I have to read the whole Bible, at least once, all the way through. No problem. I had done that a few times already. Plus, the Bible is a great read! I also have to attend the Apostolic Doctrine class with Elder Raydor Johnson of Greater Bibleway (where Bishop Ira Combs presides) and pass it. I ended up testing out with 94% without taking the class. Next, I have to attend Minister's Classes and meetings. I have to preach a 3-minute sermon, and if I'm good enough, then I get to preach a 5-minute sermon (lol… whatever). Oh, and on watch night, or some call it "New Years Service," I get a 7-minute sermon in front of the whole congregation (ok).

## EPIPHANY

After that, once I've shown myself to be "worthy," I fill out a form that has to be signed by my pastor to say I am eligible to get my "fellowship" papers. These papers mean I am certified to "minister" in my local assembly. But I have to take a test that is worded in the most confusing way to get my "fellowship" papers. These tests are conducted only once a year at the June Councils.

After that, I must hold these papers for at least a year in good standing before I am eligible to attend Aenon Bible College to obtain my minister's license. So I pass the Aenon Bible College course and the final at the next June Council a year later. Then, I must bring all my paperwork from all the above to have it verified and get my licenses sent to me by mail.

Whew! Now am I a minister? What if I didn't pass all those obstacles? Would that have made me not a minister? God forbid. I promise none of that process taught me to be a minister, nor the meaning of ministry. What it *did* do was show everyone else I "fulfilled" what was required to go on to speak to those in this organization—or at least, with this set of watchmen who were stewards of ABBA's people. It was to make sure we were all on one accord.

## Hebrews 7:25

> Wherefore he is able also to save them to the uttermost that come unto God by him, seeing he ever liveth to make intercession for them.

Who *did* teach me ministry was my God—The Great I AM, Jesus Christ (in Latin) Himself—, the Word of God, and a few key people: Bishop Willie Burrel Sr (love), Eld. Jesse Ross (prayer), Bishop Norman L. Wagner (anointing), psalmist Mitchell Jones (forgiveness), Marvin Sapp and MaLinda P. Sapp (purpose), and Pastor Larry Clifton (the rightly dividing of the Word of God).

But while I was attending U of M, God would express to me what ministry truly is. I was going there to get my degree, but God was showing me what the "church" had become: wretched, miserable, poor, blind, and naked. God calls this Laodicea (Revelations 3:14-22). And I was to be the opposite. You see, on my way to class, I would be at the city bus stop in the blistering cold winter air. I would see so-called-saints drive past me, honk their horn, and wave at me while going in the same direction but never stopping to offer me a ride.

Then, if I happened to make it to "church" on Sunday to rest from my studies, I would be greeted with, "I saw you at the bus stop!", "Where have you been?" or "Are you still saved?" Not a warm, "How are you?", "I missed you!" or "Let me know what you need." Many would ignorantly smile as they judged my lack of attendance at "church" as me being a backslider in my pursuit of higher learning. But they would have thought me wrong if I had identified their lack of charity as the same (Colossians 3:12-14; I Peter 4:8; I John 3:17, 18).

I remember asking, "God, if you bless me with a car, I promise I will turn NOT one person down for a ride." God blessed my mother to be able to get $5,000 to get me a car. I got a 1991 Ford Escort. God blessed this little red car so much that it would ride a week on "E" but would not die. It's only because I kept the promise I made to God and did NOT deny one person in need of a ride. More so, HE kept HIS promise to me since "before the foundation of the world." Because Abba "foreknew." Amen.

I remember one time I came to a Sunday church service. I sat in the balcony so I could leave as soon as church let out to avoid all the ups and downs that sometimes came with talking to people after church. I sat there thinking, "This can't be all to salvation?" To come to a building, hear a preacher of motivation compelling us to continue to come back because "God has another word for [us]" (maybe only retaining 20% of the message), singing songs, trying to jam, trying to sound the best, or "killing it" (calling it praise) and doing the same thing next week.

It wasn't all bad, but the monotonous routine of nothing more than shouting and screaming, proclaiming God was in the place with no transformation of anything, was like an alarm clock, warning me this wasn't all good either. I was reading passages in the Bible concerning the actions of Jesus and comparing them to what we, as an assembly, were doing.

After the service, someone said, "Wasn't that message good today?!!" At first, I felt awful because I had missed the message, having drifted off into my own study. I asked, "Help me, which part of it was best?" The person replied,

"Well, all of it, but it got hype when he talked about the Name! You know there is something about that Name, 'Jesus'!" After they said that, I didn't feel so bad; they had clearly missed the message too! I went to an elder of the church and told him that I had been studying during the preaching, and I felt kind of bad. He said, "It's not your fault you're bored."

I *was* bored. I was bored of their indifference. What I was experiencing paled in comparison to what I knew about God, like the difference between hamburger and steak; rap and hip hop, or the NBA players and Michael Jordan.

I needed more, and I couldn't get it where I was, so I left on a "sabbatical," if you will, in search of "The More." Some would label me a "church hopper" at this time in my life as I searched for "The More." "The More" is what I had when I was 5 years old, sitting on the lap of Pastor Elder Jesse Ross as he read scriptures to me, receiving the baptism in Jesus' Name. And when I was 6 years old, and I received the spiritual baptism of the Holy Ghost with the evidence of speaking in other tongues as the Spirit gave utterance.

The difference between me and a church hopper was that I didn't move from church to church because I was mad at the pastor or didn't get my way; I was on a quest. I questioned and answered questions, visiting many different religions, using the Bible as my guide for comparing truth.

Later in my life, my God, Abba Father, would reveal to me, "You are here at Lighthouse Church because God sent you to be a prophet in this house." And by the way, Abba also proclaimed by the guest prophet, "Don't worry about all the churches you attended; I sent you to those as well." I jumped off the floor where I was hiding in worship to run in praise as I heard Prophet Todd Hall speak my name, "MarShon," before belaying the words of the Most High in the most prophetic way. Thank you, Abba. And thank you, Prophet Todd Hall, for your sacrifice.

I would soon learn why there are so many factions of Christianity and other religions. It always came down to the interpretation of certain words in one's religious book. Abba reminded me of the Garden of Eden, how the serpent changed the sentence God spoke into a lie just by adding one little three-letter word to the sentence: the word "not." From God saying, "… in the day that thou eatest [of the tree of the knowledge of good and evil] thou shalt surely die," to the serpent saying "Ye shall not surely die."

Many religious sects add their own words to try explain God's Word. And by doing so, they change the Word of God into a lie, gaining their just reward (Revelation 22:18, 19). This is a perfect example of how all have sinned and fallen short of the glory of God. Many have tried to interpret the Bible with their intellect instead of allowing God to reveal Himself in due season.

1 Corinthians 1:18-21 says:
18 For the preaching of the cross is to them that perish foolishness; but unto us which are saved it is the power of God.
19 For it is written, I will destroy the wisdom of the wise, and will bring to nothing the understanding of the prudent.
20 Where is the wise? Where is the scribe? Where is the disputer of this world? Hath not God made foolish the wisdom of this world?
21 For after that in the wisdom of God the world by wisdom knew not God, it pleased God by the foolishness of preaching to save them that believe.

MARSHON PEOPLES

# BULLET TWENTY

EPIPHANY

In 1999, I felt led to start a non-profit organization called "Inspirational Youth for Christ (IYFC)." IYFC was formed to empower any and all God-inspired gifts of the youth by providing an outlet and platform to showcase their talent to various multimedia companies.

Inspirational Youth for Christ (IYFC) logo

The true thought behind IYFC was for youth to be employed by these multimedia companies for being who God designed them to be. Imagine that! Getting paid to be you! How hard is it to gain wealth doing what you love, being who you are, and what God purposed you to be?

At the time, I couldn't afford any help, like a lawyer to help me write and get a non-profit 501(c)(3) status. I went to different people asking for money to help me get my 501(c)(3), and no one would. At the time, I was working for Eric and Tandra at Puffer Reds, an urban store. Definitely a staple in the community of Ypsilanti, Michigan. And I kept writing out my plan while stacking clothes and helping customers. I was earning money at the hottest clothing store in town. I met a few stars there as well. One of the groups I met was 702. They came during the promo of their album. You can still go there today to get the latest urban-style clothing and see some of the legendary historical moments captured on their walls.

I appreciated the job at Puffer Reds. It was decent money, and I was broke. I was working at Eastern Michigan University as a janitor while still attending The University of Michigan at the same time, but that Eastern janitor job abruptly ended. Everywhere I went to get a job, they told me I was overqualified when they would see the University of Michigan on my resume.

EPIPHANY

My uncle, Bruce "Randy" Calloway of Calloway Masonry Contractors, did have some construction work for me though. I appreciate everyone who helped me at this time in my life.

One day I sat in the Ypsilanti Library on Whitaker Road, and I started digging up all these books concerning non-profits and how to form a 501(c)(3) non-profit organization, in order to do what I felt led to do in the community. I read book after book, wrote program after program, and finally turned everything in. It took another 6 months for me to get my non-profit status! When it finally arrived, I was so excited. I did it only with and by the grace of God.

The IYFC board was phenomenal. It featured Karl Reid (from Commissioned), Greg Peoples (Eastern Michigan University Dean of Students), Lynn Dumas (University of Michigan Dean Assistant), Ted Schrork (Vice President of Citizens Banks), Ann Marie Damon (March of Dimes), Brenda Byrd (Music Director of Messias Temple) and Robert Walker (Wise Steward Ministries; I even helped him with his own non-profit status).

The motto of IYFC was "Create a better future by doing NOW!" I wanted to do just that: change the youth's futures for the better by unlocking who they are through their gifts. But as always, when people don't understand the vision, they do their best to kill it. Proverbs 29:18 says, "Where there is no vision, the people perish: but he that keepeth the law, happy is he."

There are so many times that God has delivered me from some type of trouble or danger, seen and unseen. At this time, I was driving for Golden Limousine. My good friend Sean Duval was the owner, and I was driving one of the Town Cars. I had just dropped off a high-profile client at Hart Plaza in Detroit and was heading back on 94. This was during the Winter. It was really cold that day, and as I was driving on the highway, my Town Car hit some black ice. The car began to fishtail.

Golden Limousine had trained us very well on how to maneuver and how to get control of the car, but it was so much black ice that my car slid into the middle median. It was so much snow, too, that it created a snowbank in the form of a ramp on the median strip.

# EPIPHANY

My car rolled up the ice like a skateboard, went up into the air, and came back down like a ramp at a skate park. At that point, the car was facing oncoming traffic, and everyone else had stopped. ALL I can remember is saying, "Ah!!!" That was all I could get out, but Abba interpreted it as, "Help!" I am still here today to tell you about that story. The car literally had basically turned upside down, but God turned it right back—right side up! Thank you, once again, my ABBA.

The good thing about working for Golden Limousine was that I did get a chance to meet a whole bunch of stars: Danny Glover, Barry Sanders, Stone Cold Steve Austin, Tommy Hearns, Slick Rick, Henry Kissinger, Tony Delk, Jason Kidd, Jake Tsakalidis, Donnie McClurkin and all the Pistons—Rip, Mateen, Big Ben, Sheed, Billups and The Prince of the Palace, Tayshaun.

One day I was sent to pick someone up at the Palace, and when I got to there, it had Jake Tsakalidis and another player by the name of Dawaun as the players on my order. It was "As Directed," meaning you take the rider wherever they ask to go, and I had to go to the garage of the

Palace. So, I parked in the garage, and I was standing there with my sign for the longest time. I finally went up to the window and said, "I'm looking for these two passengers," and security looked at the card and said, "Oh, those two are in the game. You have to wait 'til after the game before they come out. This is the tunnel, and the game just started. I tell you what you do, you walk down this tunnel, and the usher will show you a seat."

I couldn't believe it! I was sitting courtside. The usher asked, "Would you like anything to eat?" I said, "Burger and fry and a Coke." Lo and behold, I didn't have to pay for the burger, the fries, *or* the Coke. Nor did I have to pay for all the shrimp and all the goodies in the locker room and the Palace. I didn't have to spend any of my money that day; the ball players' manager took care of it all.

On top of that, I got a $100 tip from the manager, who so graciously left it on the floor of my Town Car. I said, "The gratuity is included!" But he just smiled and threw it on the floor anyway. What I really felt like using it for was clothes! It was an awesome day. Won't He do it! Shout out to Sean Duval and Golden Limousine in Saline, Michigan.

EPIPHANY

# BULLET TWENTY ONE

Many people were very interested in a program launched by IYFC in 2004 called Project "SING." Oh, let me tell you... this made a lot of noise in different cities—Detroit, Chicago, Cincinnati, and Windsor, Canada! It even made it in the Ypsilanti Press, our local back then. Although the title read "Motivational Youth For Christ" instead of "Inspirational Youth For Christ." Unfortunately, in my own town, people I knew and some I loved would not support Project "SING." I know of some (who shall remain nameless) went as far as to bad-mouth the project to others in other cities to stop it from progressing!

At the time, Mitchell Jones from Commissioned was working on a solo project, and I helped road manage some of his traveling events with his cousin, Rochelle Mann. Mitchell Jones had ministered to me in an uttermost way with late-night sessions in his recording studio, just breaking down scripture and enjoying revelations in song.

I invited Mitchell Jones and Third Dimension to come to Ypsilanti to do a worship service. This service was marketed to the fullest! Even though this was an awesome all-star evening, and the worship was powerful, many did not show.

# EPIPHANY

This devastated me. It wasn't the *idea* people didn't want to support; they just didn't want to support *me*. But not coming together to worship? I can't understand that. Why is it that people fight it when you try to do something great to help others!? But when you're not doing anything at all, they talk about you. It's almost as though people settle for mediocrity and want you to settle, too. They want the credit for your idea but don't want to do the work. Some even went so far as to mimic the concept, called theirs something different, and turned their backs on me. As if we never had a conversation about working together. However, in all of this, the Most High was persecuted too. Amen.

So gears shifted. Like a ram in the bush, we revamped and launched a new project from IYFC called Nikeo Sports. Nikeo Sports was an AAU basketball program that, in addition to basketball, taught life skills, such as stock investment, money management, tutoring, SAT pre-testing, and included a summer job program. It was very successful; 227 youth tried out, and 90 youth made the teams throughout the program during the first year!

What God did through me was have college students who were going for their teaching certificate tutor my AAU basketball team. I paid a certified teacher to be present so the college students could get their credits. They got credit by tutoring my AAU boys for better grades, and the teacher still got paid to teach. It was a win-win-win situation for everybody who participated. I extended this program to the Grand Rapids area while living in the city by establishing the I AM a Son© mentorship program. But, yet again, there are always those who don't see that we are all ONE.

It was at that time I felt the transformation from minister to pastor. Again, an office I reluctantly accepted. However, God has a way of persuading His sons who love Him to obey.

# EPIPHANY

MARSHON PEOPLES

# BULLET TWENTY TWO

# EPIPHANY

As you all know, I grew up in the church, and growing up in the church had its very funny moments—especially dating in the church. It was like a balancing act on a tightrope. There is always a plethora of choices, but at the time I wasn't trying to make that choice. I wanted to do it the right way, at least what I thought was right at the time. I was just in the Word, enjoying being who I was, doing my best to stay out of trouble and be a good Christian. That wasn't always easy. We like who we like, but in the church, it's way different than anywhere else.

Being single in the church, I was thrown into different categories of opinions based on how the person felt about me. Some opinions were formed whether they knew me or not. My Mom raised me to be clean, dress nice, fix my hair, and smell good. Growing up, she also called any female who called the house looking for me "stanky," lol! She would say, "Some stanky girl called you."

No name, no number, and there wasn't any email or text then. I now know why I was told, "Just keep living." Anyway, lol!

A simple "hello" was like a marriage proposal in church. Lol! Seriously, I couldn't have a simple conversation in the hallway with any female unless it was a momma, grandma, or great aunt-type. And some of those were "set ups" for their young lady family member. Lol! Couldn't hardly talk to anyone or just be cordial without a, "Y'all talking?", "Y'all go together?", "Y'all would make a cute couple."

Or how about this one: "You should like her." Lol, "Okay... can I learn more about her first?" Then you have that "Where are you sitting?" question that lets you know, in a light way, "I likes ya and I'm sitting next to you." Yep, you've been "claimed" whether you invited it or not. Especially at the June of the P.A.W. church councils Lol!

In loving Memory of the late great Craig Tyson Sr., Music Director of the Michigan State choir. He taught us songs in such a way that it would be the night before—or THAT day—and he would lead us in such a way that, I promise you, it was like we had been singing it for years! He was just that good.

I used to escape to the Michigan State choir councils during this time, especially if I saw Marvin Sapp or Deitrick

Haddon walk through the church doors. I knew that the State choir was going to rock that night. This was well before either of them were the pastors and recording artists they are today. It was a treat to hear the raw talent of those two powerful worshippers.

So, I could escape by wearing my all-black, learn the songs we were singing that night on the fly… lol, and jump in the NDCPYPU Michigan State choir. Yep! And don't let big bro Tyrone Kaiser get up there too! I don't have to worry about nobody trying to sit next to me now! Escape drama, lol!
I remember complimenting Bishop on his outfit (and y'all know he was always sharp!) and he said, "The Man makes the clothes look good, the clothes don't make the man." A pure gentleman. Thank you so much, Bishop, for your example!

I remember when I first learned I went on a date. A pastor told me I was on a date. Lol. For real! I had met a friend at Big Boy next to the church one night after service. He said, "When you are on the phone, you are talking, that's just talking. But once you go out to be seen in public, that's a date."

~ Bishop Gary "Cool Walk" Harper

MARSHON PEOPLES

*I Won't Complain*
Bishop William C. Abney

So I followed the Pastor's (now Bishop's) advice and took the friend out on a "real" date. I'd been on plenty of dates at this point. It's just this was someone I looked up to and I was learning what *they* meant when they said "date" and what *I* interpreted as a date were two different things.

I didn't spend a lot of money on this date. It was more like a "trust friendship" date. I asked her if she trusted me. She said, "Yes," so I asked her to close her eyes so she could "guess the experience." She closed her eyes, and I had her guess the taste of a chocolate sundae and the smell of some perfume at the mall (then got a sample to maybe buy a small bottle later on). As she smelled the scent, she murmured, "Mmmm, that smells good."

We went on walking through the mall with her still blindfolded. She flailed her hands and arms all around in a funny gesture as she tried to feel where she was. I kept asking, "Do you know where you are?" as she continued

flailing... lol. People at the mall watched with smiles as my silly blindfolded friend guessed that we were in the mall. When we arrived at our final stop, she opened her eyes to a visual of a movie called "Drumline." We kept it simple. However, even that came with its rumors! Lol!

Going out in groups is fun, but that, too, backfired on me... lol. I got in trouble for going on a date without knowing I was on a date again! Just pay attention to the seating arrangement before you sit down. You might have a prearranged seat just for you. It's a trap... It's a trap like in the movie *Predator 2* with Danny Glover. Lol.

Let's not forget about "The Infamous Plate." You church folks know what I mean. You didn't ask for it or hint at it, but when you heard, "I brought you a plate." Man, I kinda felt like Tupac: "All Eyez On Me." Lol! If I accept "The Infamous Plate" then that's automatic marriage. No proposal, no courtship; "The Infamous Plate" *is* the courtship. Yooou's married now!

Older brothers in the church would see me in the bathroom and start in too: "I see that gal done brought you plate," in that Elder McMurray voice. The next thing I know, I'm

getting advice about it. It would have been nice to know "The Infamous Plate" was so... infamous beforehand Oh, let's not get it twisted, young men. We all have that one (or a few) that we "shot that shot" with but "missed" and couldn't get that one that was really on the heart. I believe this is our Abba Father's way of teaching us a lesson not to put anyone before Him.

## Matthew 6:33

> But seek ye first the kingdom of God, and his righteousness; and all these things shall be added unto you

When a young woman is not interested in you, then she is NOT interested. Her body, countenance, and demeanor will say, "NO, THANK YOU." Just listen carefully. You'll hear the difference between "try harder" and "get away." And don't try to figure out why she doesn't like you. She might not know herself. Or she just doesn't like your vibe.

If you try to find out from her why she doesn't like you before she is willing to share, you might make matters worse and lose a friend in the process. Perceptions and misunderstandings can cause harm in friendships. Let your actions speak for you. Move on to building your dream. ~ Blessings

## ADVICE DISCLAIMER

> For those individuals who are focused, listening for the Father's voice, need a little space to hear Him or to think, and don't want to hurt anyone. When you visit any assembly at home or abroad, sit in the very front, next to the exit or the pastor. This tempers a lot of misunderstandings.

MARSHON PEOPLES

# BULLET TWENTY THREE

# EPIPHANY

One of the problems I had growing up in the church was that many people wanted to push me toward what they saw in me instead of allowing God to manifest and reveal His anointing to me in His perfect season. I knew I was being called to pastor, but I ignorantly tried to run to the backside of Detroit, where no one really knew me, to a church called Daystar.

A friend of mine named Angela attended Daystar, where her father was the presiding apostle—Apostle Ellis Smith. The pastor was a young, anointed man. He was my age but operated under a different anointing than me. His name is Pastor Ken Howard. From the first day I arrived, God began to do His work in me.

The usher was a seasoned mother of the church. She was from the old school—she discerned what I was. The elderly usher said to me, "You belong up front." I replied, "No, ma'am, I would like to sit more in the middle." She commanded me in that old, strong, grandmotherly way, "No, you are a minister, and you belong up front!"

I tried once again to place myself in a blended area. The regal usher responds, "Young man, you are a minister, it's all over you, and you belong up front! Now come on!" I was very uncomfortable, but I obeyed the usher. I sat down.

The worship was something wonderful that is hard to explain. It was a sound of reverence and purpose. There was this surrendering posture in the songs. One said, "Better is one day in Your courts, better is one day in Your house, better is one day in Your courts than a thousand elsewhere…" The way the worship team sang the song unveiled an opening, like a spiritual door for me to walk through.

Not too long after this, Apostle Smith had me pray over the offering. After I prayed… he began to speak over my life, saying, "Your mouth just betrayed you. I see the apostolic mantle resting upon you. God is going to operate through you like never before. He called you to a powerful anointing." I stood there, knowing this man could not have spoken to anyone I knew. I knew God was speaking.

During another service, the youthful, anointed Pastor Ken Howard called me to the front. "Walk through that wall," he said. I looked at him, hesitated for a moment, then began to walk through the wall. But Pastor Ken told me to stop and come back. Then he said, "This is how you do God; you hesitate when He speaks, and God wants you to submit."

In yet another service, Pastor Tim Alden from California came to town. Again, the worship was powerful. Pastor Tim was prophesying over people he had called up or who had come to the altar for prayer. But I didn't move; I stayed in worship. This time, Pastor Tim pulled me to the front. I was thinking, "Lord, this man doesn't know me, and I will walk out of here immediately."

God spoke through Pastor Tim in a slight song as that sound of reverence went forth. He said, "I've called you to be a watchman in the house, a watchman on the wall. I've given you eyes to see the days ahead for decisions you need to make—career decisions. Listen, the priestly anointing is resting on you like never before. He is giving you a greater revelation and greater understanding. The priests, when they were unable to decide matters, would bring the matters before the Urim and Thummim. Which means they bathe decisions in Light. Which is what you have to do. No decision you make can be taken lightly; every decision you make is very, very important and must be strategic. Then God is going to take you higher and higher!!" This... needless to say, floored me. I lay on the floor in front of the altar at Daystar Church with tears streaming down my face and asked God to forgive me for my foolishness in thinking I could run from my calling.

To understand ministry, one has to understand the concept and the demonstration of love. Love is denying oneself for the sake of another.
~ M.K. "The Miracle" Goode-Peoples

EPIPHANY

# BULLET TWENTY FOUR

# 1

John 3:16 says, "Hereby perceive we the love of God, because He laid down His life for us: and we ought to lay down our lives for the brethren."

Over the years, our core group of brotherhood grew. We even call ourselves The FIRM, originally coined by Kevin Toney when he was younger. He gave us all nicknames of his choosing. We even had our own "spot" where we'd go to eat—Pizza Papalis in Greektown, Detroit. We would go on many outings and have fun going to gospel concerts, plays, and festivals. We would even go to some of the gospel recording artists' houses to fellowship—and still do.

We're a group of brothers from the same assembly, bred to be leaders in the Most High, each in his own strengths. That's pretty much it! All are connected through and to music in some way or the other. ABBA Father used Kevin to pick a powerful roster. ~ Blessings

Abba often showed Himself strong in those times as well. He provided for us from dangers, seen and unseen, repeatedly. There were a lot of times, too, when we weren't necessarily facing any danger. It was more like... should I say, my Abba Father showing off? There was this time we were going to the Motor City Bowl game up at Ford Field, and it was so difficult finding a place to park. I was driving, and looking, and looking... Bo was with me. Eventually, I said, "You know what? I'm a child of the King!"

So I turned my car around to find a closer park. Lo and behold, there was one park left! All the other parks that were full cost about $20 to even $35. But in this park, there was this spot just sitting right there, close to the Ford Field, with this guy monitoring the parking lot. I asked, "Is that my spot?" He replied, "For $10 it is!" I said back, "Then let me in then!!!" in a real high-pitched voice like Chris Tucker. Bo and I laugh about that to this very day!

MARSHON PEOPLES

# BULLET TWENTY FIVE

# EPIPHANY

In 2007, the housing market changed for the worse. This had a significantly adverse effect on what I was trying to accomplish in the community. By then, I was 32 years old. My biological father and I had met three years prior. We had a genuine friendship, but at the time, we had not yet fully formed that father-son bond. Because of my real estate knowledge, he invited me to come live with him so I could help him sell his home. He wanted to move to Baton Rouge, Louisiana, for a trucking opportunity. So, I moved to Grand Rapids.

My feelings toward my father were becoming stronger and more endearing due to the nature of the invite. I was excited! It was a restart and a new beginning if you will. It sounded like a good idea at the time. My father had a fiancé (now since divorced) who lived with him already and didn't like the idea of moving so far from her adult children and grandchildren.

On one particular day, my father was sharing how he was trying to figure out how to get the money to buy a truck in the hopes of making even more money. This was his attempt to avoid moving to Baton Rouge since this out-of-state trucking opportunity displeased his fiancé.

I saw my move to Grand Rapids as an opportunity to help him and his fiancé in their dilemma. Using my real estate knowledge, I approached my father with a sensible plan. He loved it! But he said, "I need you to explain this to my fiancé." I was preparing to go preach at the Guiding Light Mission Homeless Shelter that evening. I thought this would be a quick presentation, which my father and his fiancé could discuss once I had left.

The plan for my father to stay in Grand Rapids and for his fiancé to stay near her grandchildren was simple to me and carried a low risk. I asked my father, "How much will you make with your own truck?" He told me, "$3,000 per week." I shared the plan for him to take $7,000 equity from their house and put it down on a $28,000 used diesel semi-truck. With a $3,000 weekly income, he could quickly pay his equity back.

DISCLAIMER: I am not a real estate broker. Examine interest rates, prepayment penalties, and type of loan with a professional licensed broker in your state. Now, you're welcome.

Unfortunately, the conversation took a bad turn. I was sent on my way to go preach my assignment. My father came to hear me preach that evening to the homeless, which I thought was thoughtful, and I loved him for supporting me in that way. But to my dismay, it was also to deliver the harsh news: I was being expelled from my father's home. I thought I was helping. More things were said, which devastated me. I choose to omit that part from this manuscript. Since then, our LOVE has grown.

I sat in my car, numb, speechless, and dumbfounded. Not knowing I was preaching to myself when I was preaching to the homeless. But my Heavenly Father, who has been there for me countless times in my life, came through yet again and comforted me with a whisper. "Remember... Remember what I have already done for you in your future." God brought to my remembrance Hebrews Chapter 4, which speaks of the work having been "finished since the foundation of the world"... and His "rest."

My big sister, Tonya, and her husband at the time, Corey, took me into their home. This was a huge gesture, considering their townhouse-style apartment only had two bedrooms and a basement.

They had four children and two dogs. Adding me into the mix, we had our own version of *The Brady Bunch* or *Good Times*. God blessed some special people to come into my life for a season and "restore" me in the most powerful way to get me back on my feet. I will always appreciate and love my sister, her husband, my nieces, and my nephew for their sacrifice and blessings. God bless you. Amen.

God speaks to me to write the vision and make it plain upon tables... For three days, He reveals a ministry to me that He will have me pastor called "BEYOND." He instructs me on every minute detail of what to do. Now it's just a matter of when. God has already called me to pastor and given me the vision for the ministry... so what's next?

# EPIPHANY

The year is 2008. In 4 years, I will meet the designated bullet I call Epiphany. Epiphany will shake the country. As the "shot heard 'round the world" started the revolutionary war, so will Epiphany spark a movement of "revelation" called BEYOND. Many people will marvel at the miracle God will do for me because I will go beyond and back. I will survive.

MARSHON PEOPLES

# BULLET TWENTY SIX

# EPIPHANY

I've had my share of women in my life that I thought, maybe... you know... might be the one. Some thought they were the one as well. I would ask men who had been married for 20-plus years how they knew their wife was the one. All these men would answer the same: "You just know." I knew whoever my wife was, she would have to understand my calling to ministry and enhance me as I enhanced her.

On October 31, 2008, I met Heavenly. Her name alone was befitting to what I saw. What's even more astounding, it was the day after my spiritual birthday, October 30, 1980. Yet another powerful gift from my Lord Jesus. Not only was she the most beautiful sight to me, but she would appeal to my spiritual stance on life too. This was most important to me. We spent countless hours learning from one another. So the obvious conclusion to me was... "She is," so I thought, "the one."

To cap it off, her birthday is the same day as mine, August 21. But I'm 4 years older than her. I found myself holding back my feelings, not knowing if she felt the same. We would talk on the phone for hours.

I would ask her to go for dinner with me, watch movies, or just chill. I was captivated by her ways, her drive, and her smile. What I admired most was that she was on the same page that we weren't going to breach God's Word.

One night after, meeting at the movies and seeing our chosen feature, we sat outside in the parking lot, listening to old-school hits and enjoying ourselves 'til like 3am. One evening after her recording session, she called and asked if she could stop by for me to have a listen to her newly recorded rap song. I didn't know she felt the same as I did. The song's chorus was, "I think that you could be the one." I thought she was referring to God until I heard the verse, "I love it when you pray, we're born on the same day..." my heart's delight revealed... Heavenly was referring to me as her husband.

I did my best to maintain my cool, masculine, chill façade, but when I excused myself from her presence, I am not too ashamed to admit I did the jackpot "cha-ching!!" gesture with a giddy Kool-Aid man cheesy smile before I regained my resolve and returned to my Heavenly guest.

# EPIPHANY

We were wedded on May 1, 2009. It was a small, intimate wedding with our most intimate circle of friends and family. I wanted it to be special, so of course, I asked (now Pastor) Larry Clifton to administer the Holy wedding ceremony. Heavenly and I were officially ready to embark on our new journey of God-willed ministry.

Since then, things have changed. However, I've learned we ALL have choices in life, and Abba doesn't choose for us. Abba Father sets a predestined path for us according to His will, and we choose whether or not to follow that path. And some friendships stand the test of time.

MARSHON PEOPLES

# BULLET TWENTY SEVEN

# EPIPHANY

During this time in my life, I was working at the Seidman Boys and Girls Club in Grand Rapids, MI, serving in a few capacities. Working there, I developed many relationships with the youth in the city of Grand Rapids. I also learned about the personal needs of families in general.

While others seem to take a stance of "this is just my job," I, on the other hand, looked at this position with the Boys and Girls Club as my ministry. My reason for working there was to transform lives. I learned my biggest strength was also my biggest weakness... I cared too much. My passion to do more and my relationship with God seemed to isolate me from the other workers. The office at the Boys and Girls Club seemed to be filled with fun and laughter—that is, until *I* walked in. It was a very lonely and awkward feeling. So, I spent most of my time mentoring, conversing, and empowering the youth there.

One day, while serving, when I had first started at the Club, a young teenager named Shakur asked me to be his and his friends' basketball coach. Shakur was in the eighth grade as a Rising Star.

He and his friends wanted to play up in the Boys High School Night Court League at this recreation center called The Paul I. Phillips Building, which I would later learn was the main event at that time in Grand Rapids. This was an all-city bragging rights venue.

Shakur and his friends didn't know that I was a real basketball coach for years with my own AAU organization in Ypsilanti—Nikeo Sports—various AAU basketball organizations like Big Eekay Sports, as well as coaching clinics. I asked young Shakur, "What made you ask me to coach this team?" His answer was simple. "Because I like you." So I asked him to let me meet the team.

I asked the rag-tag bunch of misfits if they wanted a mentor coach or if they wanted to win. They all replied, "We want to win!" I asked, "Are you sure? Because that's two different coaches." They said they wanted to win. I looked at the group of boys and said, "Okay, but you have to do what I tell you for a chance to win." And they agreed. They all had some skill, given the fact that we were in the hood, so most kids there get the general idea. But to win, they must be a team. And my new team had a prior coach in John Lamarr, who I would later meet at one of the Paul I. Phillips basketball games. We became close coaching mates, even to this very day.

I worked this band of naïve eighth graders hard to get them ready for their older high school challengers. However, these boys also needed a mentor. They named our team "Thicker Than Water." We would contest the local high school teams that Summer. We also played in the AAU tournaments and competed against other Boys and Girls Clubs of West Michigan. With my prior coaching experience, I knew I wanted to empower them with more than basketball. And since they wanted to win, I had to get them to work together. The concept is called RESPECT.

Shakur Sanders, Ryan Anderson, Kevin Smith, Antonio McKinney, Troncé Rienstra, Dareon Buckner, Jimmy "Hairline" Braxton, JW, and Rahiem Jones were the original team members. We were winning game after game.

I noticed people started treating us like we were villains. Even the ticket lady at the entrance to Paul I. Phillips chimed in, "Y'all are going to lose today against this team." I asked, "Why are you saying this?" I couldn't understand why people were against my boys.

She replied, "Y'all ain't played nobody." In my mind, we already won because my boys were getting better, and everyone they played was "somebody" because, remember, these boys were in the eighth grade playing up in the High School League. Well, needless to say, we won that game as well. All praise to the Most High. To God be the glory!

We were undefeated most of the summer and took second place in the Paul I. Phillips High School Night Court League, only to lose to the well-renowned Ottawa Hills High School basketball team. Antonio McKinney even got the "Big Man" of the year award as an eighth grader!

The very next year, EVERYONE made their respective high school basketball teams! I am still very proud that they also wanted to try again in the Paul I. Phillips Night Court tournament. By that point, we had a target on our backs. Other teams were stacking the deck to beat the ninth grade Thicker Than Water team.

I remember that second year was pretty much like the first year, but two other teams came extremely prepared: the Ottawa Hills High School varsity basketball team and another team who went and got a D1 college recruit from

Providence to play with them. They even had one of my players on their team who had chosen to leave us. Maybe he believed we would lose. But he knew our plays. This was a problem for me because this player was good at stealing the ball for us; now he was on the other team, where he definitely utilized his skill set.

It was a packed house at both of those games. In the game with the D1 recruit, I can remember referees even saying before the game, "They're going to try to cheat y'all today." This made John Lamarr furious when he found out who was on the other team. One of our former players and the D1 recruit who was already playing for his respective collegiate team. John went to the director of the league, basically to ask him what was going on. The director even tried to leave, with John following him outside to continue to plead our case and to get an answer for the main question: "Why?"

We battled the super team in the packed Paul I. Phillips gym. It seemed all of Grand Rapids was there. The score went back and forth as frustrations continued to grow. Each coaching staff member of our contesting team was firing quips and intense eye gestures toward each other's benches.

I was constantly trying to work and create plays on the fly because our former player knew our strategy and plays. We fought and fought hard. Only to lose by 4 points!

Tempers were still hot after the game. Both teams were about to fight in the parking lot by our van as they were boarding to head back to the Seidman Center. I'm usually laid back, but my boys were upset. They felt cheated. They felt robbed. I intervened to calm the situation as kids and parents alike argued about the game. I made my boys shut up and get in the van to get them to safety.

I take full responsibility for the loss. I lost my focus, my calm, and my team. I allowed a matter apart from the Most High to affect my emotions. I wasn't mad for myself; it was because my boys were hurt from the start of the game. My mind was still more on "Why?" and not on intangibles to win the game. We placed second that year as well, but we made the other teams work harder than before. So really, we all won RESPECT. I am still so very proud of them. We are still "Thicker Than Water."

EPIPHANY

Some more outstanding players were added to the team in later years, and some went on to do more incredible ventures, like Porter Mayberry, currently known as "Showtime," number 0 with the Harlem Globetrotters; Joseph Hicks, currently a professional boxer on the Showtime Boxing network; Kevin Smith, currently owner of *616 Clothing*; and Devin Ivy, Ottawa Hills starting point guard and high prospect.

As the Thicker Than Water Seidman boys traveled to other Boys and Girls Clubs to play basketball against their respective teams, they won more first-place trophies.

These are still located in the Boys and Girls Club Seidman Center in Grand Rapids, Michigan. We later expanded to Lighthouse Church and had the "Saints" AAU basketball team through the Sports Power program, who qualified for Nationals! Thicker Than Water Sports Power AAU Basketball Team

I would later connect with many other programs and organizations. Namely, The Edge (Pastor Troy Evans), Young Life, Big Brother Big Sister, School of Hope, Mentor 1, Sportspower after-school program, Youth Unlimited, Youth for Christ, and several Grand Rapids public schools. This led to Heavenly and me starting a Sunday Bible class at the Boys and Girls Club facility. This took place during closed hours for all who were willing to learn about Jesus. We enjoyed our small beginning to what The Most High called BEYOND. Job 8:7 says, "Though thy beginning was small, yet thy latter end should greatly increase."

EPIPHANY

# BULLET TWENTY EIGHT

Once again, obedience plays a vital role when doing God's work. This burden to attend and help Lighthouse Full Life Center Church began to press heavily on my heart, but I didn't know why. And then I realized what it was: I didn't want to stop growing the ministry BEYOND. Things were coming together for us. I also did not want to attend Lighthouse as a long-time admirer of the senior pastor. I did not want being in awe of a man to hinder my ability to hear God's voice. This pastor was none other than the preacher, recording artist, and prior igniter of my journey into ministry by his "Purpose" message back in 1994 at the Indianapolis P.A.W Church Convention... Dr. Marvin L. Sapp.

As I hesitated to move, God helped me by giving me a push. I was laid off from my job at the Seidman Boys and Girls Club in January, 2010. This obviously hindered my access to the facility we would use for worship. Heavenly and I then began to fellowship where we were being led... Lighthouse Church. After visiting and observing the operation of the Lord, we joined the ministry and immediately started working with the church's youth.

Along with my many other connections in the community and many years of working with youth groups prior to this, I had the mindset to network all these pieces together. Almost like when Jesus made the fishermen fishers of men, to cast forth this net and draw as many young people as God would call unto Him. Pastor and First Lady Sapp immediately began to put things into motion as they had me send through my resumé and interviewed me so I could work within the ministry.

On August 21, 2010, First Lady MaLinda called me from her hospital bed to offer me a position, not knowing it was my and Heavenly's birthday. She spoke with such conviction and power, declaring, "Man of God!!! It is time for you to move forward in your anointing! I see you; I know who you are, preacher! You have a powerful anointing that you must operate in. I'm going to email you this job description, and I want you and Heavenly to pray over it. Then, after you get an answer from the Lord, you give me your answer!"

All I could say in return was, "Yes, ma'am." With First Lady Sapp, that's all most people could say, as she spoke with such authority and surety.

Respectfully, I never received that email. For, you see, First Lady MaLinda P. Sapp would go to sleep in the Lord on September 9, 2010. I believe my phone conversation with her was my birthday gift and confirmation from God to be who I was designed to be... a pastor.

Her death charged me with such a purpose that while many were understandably grieving the loss of First Lady Sapp, I would still operate in the community as a youth pastor. Understanding her passion was for the youth, as is mine, I had to do as she would say, "Keep it moving." I no longer expected to be hired by Lighthouse to serve in this capacity, so I sent my resumé to countless businesses and organizations to get a job. I volunteered everywhere in the hopes of obtaining a job. God would lead me to schools, houses, playgrounds, hospitals, and street corners to meet the needs of people. Job or no job, as long as I took care of His people, God promised He would take care of me and mine.

There was even this time, one night, I got a call from one of my mentees saying, "Coach! I need you to come get me!" With this low but sharp whisper of urgency. "These guys are after me, and I'm hiding behind a dumpster!"

EPIPHANY

I answered, "I'm on my way... Where are you?" My mentee replied in a shivering voice, still whispering, "I don't know. The last street I was on was Brown Street." I cautiously instructed him, "Make your way back to Brown Street. I will be driving very slow with my hazard lights blinking so that you know it's me. When you see me, run and jump into my car." My mentee agreed.

It felt like forever as I saw many young men out that night. I crept down Brown Street, acting as though something was wrong with my car, never looking directly at the very aware young residents of the area. With my door unlocked, anyone could have easily assaulted me, but my concern was finding my scared, lost mentee. Memories of my youthful experiences like this one came to mind. The feeling of helplessness in need of a rescuer to aid me. Now God uses me to be that aid.

After maybe 45 minutes of searching, I began to pray for my missing friend. My hope was that he was okay. Then all of a sudden, my passenger door flung open. The scared young man dove into my car headfirst, screaming, "GO, GO, GO, GO, GO!!!!!!" With the passenger side of my car door still flung open, I slammed my foot on the gas pedal, pinning it to the floor. Not knowing where the young man's assailants were, I checked all my rearview mirrors in multiple rapid glances as I sped away, seeing many pursuers way at the other end of the block, where we had just been.

My mentee eventually positioned himself upright in the seat and closed the passenger side door. I looked at him with concern and inquiry in my eyes. Without me having to verbally ask, he answered, "I was just with my boy, walking home, when these dudes on the porch of this one house just says, 'Get them!' So we just ran... I don't know where my boy is because we got split up somewhere!" He then asked me a question. The kind of question that I was afraid to hear. The inevitable question pierced me because it was heartfelt. It's what anyone connected with a bond would have asked... "Can we go find him?"

My heart was already racing. My mind thinking of all the possible scenarios. One thought I wanted to say, "No... Let's get you home." But what if it were me or someone close to me? Wouldn't I want someone to find me? So, once again, I go to my Rescuer, Provider, and Comforter—my God, Lord, and Savior, Jesus Christ, the Great I AM Salvation Almighty—for council.

Immediately, Matthew 25:40 came to mind: "And the King shall answer and say unto them, Verily I say unto you, Inasmuch as ye have done it unto one of the least of these my brethren, ye have done it unto me."

In that moment, I turned my car around to search for my mentee's friend. Looking back on this, I realize it was not my bravery nor any amount of love for the young men, but rather my love of God's Word, that turned me around. This turnaround was also our protection. Immediately, the young man in question was walking cautiously, looking in all directions. His face of relief was priceless as we pulled up to him, saying, "Get in."

This statement, "Get in," still resonates within me as God reaches out His hand through me to "touch" all who search for refuge in His Ark of Safety. This wasn't my first time, and definitely wouldn't be my last, to be the one these young men would call upon for help. During these times, my sense of urgency came from witnessing the horrid reality of the violence in our streets. Over time, I would have a number of young people I am connected with be incarcerated, on drugs, selling drugs, in gangs, hospitalized, and some even die. This only fuels my reason to be. I must cast my net NOT to *reach* people but to *touch* people! Only God knows which ones He has chosen. My quest is not to gain a title, position, recognition, or privileges from man. It is to win souls to the Messiah.

## Proverbs 11:30

> The fruit of the righteous is a tree of life; and he that winneth souls is wise.

EPIPHANY

# BULLET TWENTY NINE

It's January, Winter of 2012 in Grand Rapids, Michigan. My life is about to change drastically. I'm about to meet this bullet I call Epiphany. I'm working as a community empowerment staff member at the South East Community Association and as a basketball coach with Alger Middle School and Sportspower AAU Basketball Organization. I'm also the youth leader at Lighthouse Church where the gospel psalmist, Marvin Sapp, is senior pastor, and I'm working as a youth coordinator for Streams of Hope, a community center in Kentwood—a suburb of Grand Rapids. It may sound like I was doing a lot, but it didn't feel like it. It all flowed together as one job. So I went from no job to many jobs, helping young people. Won't He do it!

As a former Boys and Girls Club youth specialist and Bridging the Gap director, I'm utilizing my training to help empower the youth in this Kentwood area part of the city for positive outcomes. At this time, different groups of teens have come together as surrogate families—"gangs"—in order to protect themselves. Teenage girls are banded together to prevent attacks from girls, boys, men, and women who are trafficking teenagers. The teenage boys are doing the same—both for the same and for other reasons.

# EPIPHANY

The many relationships I formed with the youth of 2012 through my profession had me deeply involved in their personal matters. From their likes and dislikes to their triumphs and failures. From their academics to their places of worship, I was involved in many youths' lives.

I enjoyed coaching basketball the most. This was the perfect opportunity to teach life skills using the inner workings of the basketball game system. I would teach them to play as a unit like in a business, but allow them to shine in their strong suits during games. I was cool with my boys, but I was never common with them. Meaning I didn't try to fit in with them or hang out doing their things; instead, I listened to them to help them come to their own conclusions and solutions that would benefit their future. Very similar to how Brad Holman did my friends and me years prior during my youth.

We went on to win a few first-place trophies. Even my eighth grade Alger Middle School basketball team won their city-wide championship in 2010! One player, whom I coached, had a birthday coming up. He, his friends, and his teammates wanted to celebrate! Isaiah was his name. He asked if he could have a party at our Streams of Hope gym.

From previously working with The Boys and Girls Club, I understood that this particular request sounded innocent and straightforward, but based on the location, this gathering would require staff and proper planning. I was reluctant to grant the request. However, I made a deal with them. They had to complete a number of tasks before I would take the appeal to those I answered to.

I sat my young (teenage) men down and stressed to them the importance of security. I laid out the rules of the party: invitation only, no alcohol, no drugs, no sexual actions at the party, no loitering in the parking lot, and once you're in, you stay in. My young men agreed to the rules. I was kinda thinking that these boys would do the typical teenage thing, like get bored with the idea due to all the rules I gave them or think of something else to do instead. But these were boys from my AAU team—I never allowed them to quit. So, we planned it to be held at the center.

Everyone wants to have a Friday night party after a Kentwood basketball game, and this had been promised a few times before. We had planned to have Friday events after every home game to provide a safe outlet for teens.

# EPIPHANY

For Isaiah's party, I took it a step further by notifying Kentwood police in advance for additional reassurance of safety. What's more, this group of boys completed every task I asked them to do so I could turn in their request for the party.

This party... I had a strong feeling something was going to happen. Because of this, I asked for extra chaperones and security. The police were on alert and had a squad car circling the area as routine. Everything looked good on paper... but the night of this January 6, 2012, "safe haven" birthday party... I knew. I told my good friends, Dukes and Paris, that I did not want to do the party. But I had promised my boys. When mentoring youth, it is essential for me to keep my word and be consistent, or I will lose their trust and relationship.

Paris offered to come and help out. I told him, "Let's make you attentive upon need." One of my boys' mothers—a concerned parent—called and talked with me about the night's event, for assurance. She also asked me to call her in case of an emergency.

An hour before the party, as I lay on the black plush bean bag in my living room, my wife asked, "What's wrong?" I replied, "I don't want to do this party," as I had told my friends. "Well then, cancel it!!" she said. I said back to her sternly, "I can't! I gave them boys my word." We both sat there in brief silence. Then I got up and headed to go get the birthday boy.

I arrived at the promised time to pick up Isaiah. He's all excited with a grin on his face as he while prepares two big speakers for our drive to set up the party. "What up, Coach!" he jested. I replied, "Just keeping my word." Isaiah chuckled as he said, "Don't worry, Coach, nothing ever happens at my parties. Ask my mom!" I must admit, his words were hopeful. I still had that gut feeling, though; that foreknowledge-tingling feeling was very thick.

We're at the gym where the party's being held, and everything's going great! Sounds are blasting, the smoke machine adds a haze, and the colorful lights and projector show create the party atmosphere. It looks fantastic and fun! I still have this uneasy feeling. But my commitment to the youth gives me the strength to shrug it off. The night was still, with a cool crisp chill in the air.

EPIPHANY

The invited guests are arriving. The atmosphere is vibrant with the youthful excitement of the evening. The high schoolers are dressed to impress. I remember thinking, "This is a good crowd." Meaning "no troublemakers." The rest of the security team and I are still being cautious by checking the youth as they enter. The teens were having a great time. More and more parents dropped off their teens for a night of simple fun.

The teenagers are having a blast! I'm stationed outside, greeting parents as they drop off their teens. My car is strategically parked in front of the entrance to detour any attempt to rush the door. I have security keeping watch outside with me and chaperones maintaining the inside. Security and I are patting down the teenage boys, and the woman working check-in is checking the adolescent girls for any contraband of any kind. Every effort was made to ensure an attempt at a successful, safe haven event, which seemed to be going on without a hitch.

My wife texts me around 10 or 10:30pm to see how things are going. "It's cool," I reply. She was also going to chaperone but was across the street at her dad's house. I let her know I'll be shutting down the party in about 30 minutes, so there's no need for her to come. The police even do a sweep to scope the scene and determine that as all is well. I have no idea what's about to take place in the next 20 minutes. My life will be changed forever.

Just then, at about 10:30pm, eight young men approach the venue, and I hear a voice behind me coming from the door of the party with a warning... "Coach..." I turn to give attention, and the young man says, "Coach, pat them down real good before you let them in." "Don't worry," I reply. "Go back inside and have fun." The same young man immediately comes back out and warns me, "As a matter of fact, Coach, I wouldn't even let those guys in!" I alert security, "Everyone to the front." I'm focused on keeping the situation calm, trying to address the approaching young men with a cool-like vibe.

"How are you young men doing?" As I get closer, I notice these guys are older than the crowd inside. "Aww, we just came to have a lil' fun," they reply. As they get even closer, I can smell the alcohol and weed emanating from their persons. I tell the uninvited young men they're not allowed into this event for the following reason:

"You guys already have broken two rules," I say. "That's weed and alcohol." Closer, still. Now I can really smell their previous activities on their persons. They're quickly agitated, which tells me they don't have good intentions, but I still try to keep things calm by talking to them.

Laughing, I continue, "Okay, y'all look bout thirty! How old are you guys?" Their rocking side-to-side movements indicate things are potentially about to escalate. So I say, "I'll tell you what, that these are just kids inside, and this event is too young for you guys. But come back Thursday, I'll have the music blasting, basketballs out, and pizzas for your crew-" While speaking, I'm interrupted by one of the young men standing in front of me, yelling in my face. "My cousin is in there!!!!!" The situation gets serious very quickly.

This young man in particular is extremely adamant about speaking with his cousin who's inside, saying, "My cousin is in there, my cousin is in there!!!" I say to him, calmly, "You can't go in, but your cousin can come out." I turn impatiently to those peeking from inside the door, "Does anyone know his cousin?" Someone nods their head "yes" and then ducks inside with haste. Moments later, the mentioned cousin comes out and immediately says to his aggressive cousin, "Woah, yo bro!!!! I ain't even trying to mess with you right now!" It was like a fire that caught a gust of wind.

No matter the personnel and procedures applied, control was immediately lost. It was then that I knew what that thick feeling had been about. I have the officer on speed dial... I push "send," and just then, another commotion sparks to the right of me... at the entrance. One of the uninvited young men approaches and tries to get past me. I block the doorway and yell, "SHUT THE DOOR!!" I turn my head to grab the intruder, and then...

BOOM! Then... darkness... I can't see. I can't move. I feel like I'm floating. I can't hear anything... Oh! There's a sound... faint pop-like sound in the distance... Are they still shooting? Lord, not like this... not like this... Is this it? Is this how I'm about to go?... I am shot. I am shot in the back right side of my head. Lodged in my skull is a bullet. Hello, Epiphany.

# EPIPHANY

Epiphany means: "manifestation," "striking appearance," or "vision of God," which traditionally falls on January 6. This Christian feast day celebrates the "revelation" of God the Son as a human being in Jesus Christ. This is the day of the visitation of the "Magi" or kings to the Baby Jesus, bearing gifts. Today I, instead, am the one receiving a gift... The gift of LIFE.

MARSHON PEOPLES

# BULLET THIRTY

# EPIPHANY

A great peace like never before is present. This peace is like something extraordinary and pleasantly sweet. It's better than a bed comforter, like a warm blanket fresh out of the dryer, or, as Philippians 4:6 puts it: "the peace which surpasses all understanding." A dark red tint is surrounding me. I feel like I'm floating in 12 feet of water. My life flashes before my eyes… memories upon memories of my life. My upbringing was vivid, like a movie.

Acts 2:16-21 says:
16 But this is that which was spoken by the prophet Joel;
17 And it shall come to pass in the last days, saith God, I will pour out of my Spirit upon all flesh: and your sons and your daughters shall prophesy, and your young men shall see visions, and your old men shall dream dreams:
18 And on my servants and on my handmaidens I will pour out in those days of my Spirit; and they shall prophesy:
19 And I will shew wonders in heaven above, and signs in the earth beneath; blood, and fire, and vapour of smoke:
20 The sun shall be turned into darkness, and the moon into blood, before the great and notable day of the Lord come:
21 And it shall come to pass, that whosoever shall call on the name of the Lord shall be saved.

As I refuse to accept that this is my end, I begin to converse with my Maker, my Friend, and my God, Jesus Christ, YAHuSHAuAH Ha'Mishiach, i.e., The Great I AM Salvation Almighty. As I float in "nothingness," for lack of a better description, I say in my mind, "But you gave me BEYOND" (the ministry I am to start, which was given to me by God in detail while lying on my back for three days, to transform lives) ... These were the words spoken in pure thought to my God.

My consciousness is still there. I feel weightlessness, along with my innermost thoughts of my wife... "What about Heavenly?" Of course, I want to see her again, but I'm thinking, "It's too late." I start asking the Great I AM—my God—a million questions wrapped into one, or all at once. I'm not sure how much time has elapsed. Where I was, prior to awakening, there was no concept of time. This state of being is timeless.

In a moment, the Almighty answers my questions by allowing me to feel two fingers on my neck. I hear someone say, "If he would only breathe, I know he will be okay." I realize in this state of mind, my body is not breathing. My God then allows me another breath to LIVE. I hear the voice again, encouraging me: "Yes... That's right, breathe!" As I regain consciousness, I begin to see that it's Jennifer, the pregnant woman who was helping with admissions at the door of the party. She would be with me as I fight to stay awake.

"Are you married?" Jennifer asks. "Yes," I reply. "What's her name?" "Heavenly," I answer. She says to me, "That's a pretty name... Tell me about her." I begin describing how awesome my wife is to me and how fitting her name is for her. All the while, I'm fighting to stay awake. Each blink of my eyelids feels heavier and heavier. My body is very cold. My fingers and toes begin to feel numb and tingly. But Jennifer keeps me talking.

While lying on my back, I look to my left and see a familiar face. It's one of my boys that I mentor, Dequarrius. He begins to encourage me and helps me to focus by saying, "C'mon, Coach! Fight, Coach! You taught us to fight!" He also happens to be one of my former basketball players on my Sportspower AAU team. He reminds me of my chants as the team would battle talented opponents on the court, encouraging them to victory. Dequarrius is returning the favor.

He then says words that cause my eyes to tear up, even now: "You can't leave Heavenly." The name of my wife, whom I love dearly. He continues with piercing statements of connection, bond, and fear, "Fight coach... You can't leave me." I understood his plea far too well from the many talks I'd had with him. I look at him and say, "Okay... I got you." Yet another promise connecting me to purpose.

I want to give a special thanks to David London, who I just met in August 2022, ten years after this event. We were at a meeting when someone shared my story with the group. David, now 25 years old, said, "That was you?" "Yes," I responded. He looked at me like he had seen a ghost and then said, "I was there when they covered you up." Thank you so much for sharing yet another part of the blessing I didn't know... I was covered up. Hallelu YAHuSHAuAH!! ("praises to I AM Salvation Almighty" in Hebrew) Åsé Amen.

Back to the night of the party: The EMS workers have now arrived. They're asking me, "Where are you hit?" I lay there in a daze. I didn't know where I was hit. I hear them say, "There is blood everywhere underneath him." They say to me, "We will keep your head straight, but we have to turn you to see where you're hit to properly move you." "Okay," I say, still lying on my back. I feel cold and sleepy, but I'm determined to stay awake. I hear one of the EMS workers say, "Bullet is in his head."

Statistics show that approximately 20,000 people are shot in the head in the U.S. each year. Out of 20,000 people, 5% (1,000 people) survive. And of that 5%, ONLY 3% are high functioning to the extent that they can move about by themselves. That's 30 people out of 20,000. Hello, I'm MarShon Peoples, one of the 3% of the 5% survivors of a gunshot to the head.

While in the hospital before my surgery, I lay in the hospital bed wondering why I didn't see the bright light so many had spoken of before. And just then, Abba Father brought to remembrance Psalm 23:
1 The Lord is my shepherd; I shall not want.
2 He maketh me to lie down in green pastures: He leadeth me beside the still waters.
3 He restoreth my soul: He leadeth me in the paths of righteousness for his name's sake.

4 Yea, though I walk through the valley of the shadow of death, I will fear no evil: for Thou art with me; Thy rod and Thy staff they comfort me.

5 Thou preparest a table before me in the presence of mine enemies: Thou anointest my head with oil; my cup runneth over.

6 Surely goodness and mercy shall follow me all the days of my life: and I will dwell in the house of the Lord for ever. Amen.

This gave me all the confidence I needed to move forward. So much so that when the doctor came in to tell my wife and me that I had a choice to make. There was a pocket of air between the bullet and my brain, and they predicted that the air would corrode the bullet over time and kill me. The doctor went on to say, "If we leave the bullet in, you will die." I thought this was a no-brainer. I said, "Okay, doc, let's just take it out." "But wait," he said, "if we try to take it out, there's a 93% chance that you will die." But I'm still here. One of the 7%!!!

I wrote a song years ago. The chorus of the song says, "For I see... Through the clouds of despair... 'cause I know that You are there waiting for me with arms wide... For in You, Lord,

I know I can hide from the cataclysmic treachery that come against me... And in You, Lord, I know I am free... Where I found that your love is so kind... You're my LIGHT OF ETERNAL MIND."

This is so befitting because there was only a sense of thought. I saw no white light to go to... Not to take away from others who have had similar experiences. But for me, a knowing (Light) came over me... The designated bullet Epiphany's purpose is to reveal to me that "life is a moment." God reveals "I AM the way, the truth, and the life" (John 14:6). We, as "man," fill life with things that don't matter. "Mankind" is so small-minded to think survival is important, when "purpose" is what's important and the reason we "are" to begin with. The purpose is to know "Life" abundantly.

Epiphany's destination was designed by God to stop just short of entering the rest of my brain, to protect all that is *me* and all that God has put in me for... purpose. It's not enough to exist; we must know who we are in God and live doing and fulfilling His will, not our own. Live accordingly to do for Christ, thus changing someone's life for the better by meeting their needs. This is how one demonstrates Christ. Our own will is disobedient to the sacrifice of giving to others. Our society alone shows that "man" continually pushes the envelope in the name of being "free." But this only means selfishness, "primally uninhibited" or out-of-control greed.

Our purpose is to... "preach good tidings unto the meek; He hath sent [us] to bind up the brokenhearted, to proclaim liberty to the captives, and the opening of the prison to them that are bound; To proclaim the acceptable year of the Lord, and the day of vengeance of our God; to comfort all that mourn" (Isaiah 61:1,2). Life is a moment.

The story doesn't end there. It seemed like it should stop right there; it would be like this happy ending to a wonderful life. But the story continues. There was a process I found myself in.

I was in constant concert with my Abba Father. My head would hurt consistently, all day, every day. And I'm not talking about the small-time headache that Excedrin can get rid of; I'm talking about head trauma.

# EPIPHANY

The kind of head trauma that makes you desperate to escape its pain. It made me want to just sleep. I just wanted to get it over with, but getting it over with was not happening anytime soon.

So I just leaned on the Father. Doctors would often ask (at the numerous appointments I had after the shooting), "What's your pain on a scale of 1 to 10?" And while I thought that 10 was probably the right answer each day, it just seemed like it wasn't enough to describe my pain level. It turned into an 11! Sometimes it seemed like it turned into a 12, and the 12 turned into a 13... it's like I didn't know how much more pain I could take, and I would lay there in bed and pray to my God with tears streaming down my face.

During this time, I was in constant prayer, feeling trapped inside a physical being of pain I couldn't escape. It was like looking outward from the windows we call "eyes." All I felt was pain, all day, every day, but I would just lay in my Father God. This is not to make anybody feel sad in any way; it's just to show you the deliverance and triumph of God.

I was invited to do the Lord's work even in my condition. I was invited by the Doug and Maria DeVos Foundation to partake in what was called Leading a Community-Based Ministry. This is where they trained business people and pastors to exercise their gifts in the marketplace toward the people in the community. I am very thankful to Doug and Maria. Special thank you to Kari Bridgewater, another instructor of mine.

I was asked to visit different schools and speak of my testimony—of the goodness of the Lord! I was asked to come to TV shows, radio shows, and all. This helped me along in my healing, as people were inspired by Abba Father's goodness. So please don't be sad for me; I'm still moving forward. If I wasn't, you would not be reading this book.

Abba Father, the Great I AM, brought me through psychotherapy, physical therapy, occupational therapy, and cognitive therapy with the wonderful staff of Mary Free Bed Rehabilitation Hospital. He also set me free from the different medications they gave me. I was on everything from Amitriptyline to Nortriptyline, to Gabapentin to

# EPIPHANY

Acetaminophen to Ibuprofen to Vicodin to Oxycodone to Percocet... over the years, the amount of drugs the doctors had me on made me feel slow, thick, and lethargic. I relied on my God for my healing because the medications weren't doing it. They were just masking the symptoms.

After a while—I remember one morning in particular—I found myself waking up and reaching for the Vicodin bottle before I even grabbed a glass of water or used the bathroom. As I stared at the medicine bottle, I said, "Oh, no." That day, I made a commitment to my God, saying, "I will not take another one of these pills, and I will be made whole." And I meant it. I went cold turkey.

The doctors would say, "No, let us wean you off of it." I said, "You not weaning me off anything. My head hurts. I need something else, and y'all just keep doping me up. I will do it God's way, and I AM continuously declaring I AM whole. I have what I say." You have what you say according to His will. If it were not so, I would not have told you.

MARSHON PEOPLES

# BULLET THIRTY ONE

# EPIPHANY

As the years went by, the brain trauma condition and healing from another major surgery—a colonoscopy to remove diverticulitis from my colon—continued to put a strain on my marriage. At that time, I didn't feel like the breadwinner, the rock, the provider and protector that God had deemed MEN to be, as prophet, priest, and king.

My pop, Gregory Kenneth Goode, is always the life of the party! The kind of guy you'd love to hang out with! He's a great host, a sharp dresser, and a people person! Lol! He knows where all the good restaurants are too! He's taken me to a few spots. Every time I return, I think about how I can't wait to get back to some of those spots. He's the kind of guy that, if he knows you're in trouble, he knows someone who might be of some help. He's "the trucker with the stars" in the movie industry. He's met all kinds of stars, from actors and actresses to music moguls.

What I learned the most about my Pop is that when he gets an idea in his head, he sticks with it and he makes it happen. No holds barred. Once he makes up his mind, it's made up. And then he has it in his hand the next time you see him. If not, then something came up, or something else really happened that prevented him from obtaining his goal. And best believe you would hear about it too. Lol!

I remember one day when I was living with him in Atlanta. I had just had an operation to remove part of my colon. At the time, I was also still healing from the headshot wound. My wife was out of town, training for a new position at her job. I was lying in bed watching TV when all of a sudden, my body started convulsing with these sharp pains. It was like a spiky, prickly feeling all over my body. My ABBA Father stepped in yet again.

See, normally, my Pop would just let me rest and not bother me during the day. He had given up his room for me to use as I recovered. This was a big old gigantic room!!! It had a big bed, a fireplace, a walk-in closet, a big bathroom with jacuzzi-style tub... you name it! It was like its own little apartment inside the house almost. I am so honored that he did this for me. He made so many sacrifices to make sure I was comfortable.

That day, Pop came upstairs to check on me, and it turned out I really needed him. When he saw me, he asked, "Are you okay?" "Pop," I said, "something ain't right..." He

EPIPHANY

immediately helped me downstairs and into the car. Next thing I knew, we were at the hospital. It was a good thing he got to me when he did, too. We learned that my potassium levels had shot way down, and had I not gotten to the hospital when I did, I would have transitioned. I appreciate him so much for being there for me. He came to the hospital every day to see me. Yep, whenever he got the chance. Sometimes it was even more than once a day. Thanks, Pop.

I'm one of six of his sons and daughters. Altogether, in birth order, it's Tonya, Kevin, myself (MarShon), Tamara, Tremell, and Jasmine. I can honestly say that my pop made a major decision to be in all of our lives. And he's helped us all in some way, shape, form, or fashion, contributing to our dreams and pushing us forward to success. ~ Blessings, Family & as we say, "It's All Goode."

MARSHON PEOPLES

# BULLET THIRTY TWO

# EPIPHANY

I had been looking for a church home while I was healing in Atlanta. I ended up with two assemblies I could lean on: Doctors Benjamin and Sherry Gaither at Stronghold Church (I was adopted by Myrna Polk, her husband, and their family) and Apostle Buddy and Mary Crumb at Life Center Church (I was adopted by Joyce Ross, her husband, and their family).

I want to thank these two families richly from the bottom of my heart. At the time of my healing, my journey, and my recovery, my ABBA sent you two families to comfort me and give me the spiritual aid I needed in that "strange land." Thank you so very much.

These two assemblies had two very distinct modes of operations, but Abba used both places in the mightiest way. Doctors Ben and Sherry Gaither spoke to what I was to continue to do—that is, "take the Kingdom into the marketplace"—while Apostle Buddy and Mary Crumb spoke prophetically as to *how* I was to take the Kingdom into the marketplace.

Pastor Samuel of Life Center Church was the powerful pastor who asked me after attending for a while, "What are you doing here?" "I go here!" I replied. And he then rebutted, "Why aren't you out on assignment?" I looked at him, puzzled. Pastor Samuel continued to say, "I've seen you too many Sundays." Remember, where I come from, if I missed too many Sundays, I would be considered M.I.A. or out of order. But here, if you're there too many Sundays, you're not operating in who God has deemed you to be; you're only supposed to come home for a refresher.

I viewed myself as someone broken and healing. Pastor Samuel did NOT! He described the ministry I was to steward to the LETTER without seeing a website or a brochure, and I hadn't shared the vision with anyone in Atlanta. It was the same ministry Abba had me write about for three days, five years before Pastor Samuel spoke of it to me. He was describing BEYOND Christian Renaissance Movement (visit www.GoodePeoples.com)

One service, there was an elder, whom I thought was a visitor, who had come home from a sabbatical. Apostle Buddy Crum tells us to turn around and "pray" for the one behind us. I turned around to see this elder, maybe in his late 50s at the time, and we began to pray with one another.

As we were praying, he suddenly took charge and started speaking about my head. I didn't find this strange since I have a scar on the back of my head. But then he took his hand and placed it on my stomach. Mind you, I had a scar on my stomach from my colonoscopy, but there's no way he could've seen that!

This whole time, Heavenly was sitting next to me. He took my hand and put her hand into mine, and then he squeezed my hand, saying "At 2:00 am in the morning when you cannot get to sleep, God wants you to pray and talk to Him." He squeezed my hand tighter and said again, "At 2:00 am in the morning, God wants you to speak to Him in your heavenly language." He went on to proclaim, "There are two witches trying to destroy your marriage. One is light skin, and the other is dark." This floored me. It made too much sense for too many things that were presently going on. I knew God was talking to me through this man.

At the same assembly, Abba had the most unusual little boy minister to me as well. One of my White little brothers who came to me with his football. He asked me, "Will you sign my football with your favorite scripture?" I said, "Sure, if you read the scripture and tell me what it say later!"

"Okay!" he said. So I wrote on his football, "Micah 6:8," which says, "He hath shewed thee, O man, what is good; and what doth the Lord require of thee, but to do justly, and to love mercy, and to walk humbly with thy God?"

When I saw the little boy again, I stopped him in the hallway. I asked him, "Do you know my favorite scripture?" figuring he would not know who I was or even remember which scripture I wrote on his football. He said, "Yes, Micah 6:8," and then recited it word for word and ran off to continue playing.

I was very young, when Abba began to reveal the concept of TIME to me. Three years old. My mom lay me on the couch in the living room as she was on her way to work at some place called GE. I understood time in relation to the sun, by watching the shadow of the house to the sidewalk. I knew when people or a cartoon was on, based on where the shadow of the top of the house was positioned. The house faces west, so as the sun rises, the shadow from the point at

# EPIPHANY

the top of the house would lower across the sidewalk. As the sidewalk shadow would lower, a particular person would come home, or it was time to do a certain thing.

Every morning it was dark, and granddad would get up singing. Didn't matter how early he got up; he was going to sing at the top of his lungs and yawn really, really loud!!! He would come downstairs singing and cook breakfast—sausage, grits, eggs, and toast or biscuits. The sausage he would make was a spicy sausage. Either the one with a pig on the cover of the package or Bob Evans. The biscuits were always flaky, and the syrup was a syrup that, for years, we called "ALAGA surp!" Come to find out, it was actually Alabama (AL) and (&) Georgia (GA) syrup. "A.L.a.G.A." ... Lol!!! Granddad left for work every morning, saying to me, "See you later, alligator." He taught me to reply, "After while, crocodile." Love you, Granddad. "Your peanut head grandson."

I eventually mentioned the concept of time to Pastor Raydor Johnson and Elder Charles Marshall. The way I described it was like being on a car ride from Ypsilanti to Muskegon (a two-and-a-half-hour car ride). Imagine two people in the car together, but the passenger falls asleep while the driver keeps driving. During this time, the driver is still aware of time, but the one who went to sleep is not. When you get to your destination, the person who was sleeping says, "Wow! We're here already!" But the one who's been driving says, "What do you mean 'already'? It took two and a half hours to get here!" This is the concept I was referring to: the passage of time.

I was on the couch, healing, not feeling much like a king. But at the same time, as I was healing, I was learning how to get my insurance license so I could provide for my family—do something to bring in some more income so I can help out. I took a step. I did it!!! I got my insurance license. Now take another step... and another one... take another one... and each time before you take a step, ask the Father, and He will order the next step. Åsé

ATTENTION MEN: It is hard for a woman to accept a man that's down. No matter what happens to him. After a while, it hurts women to see their men down. It affects them mentally and emotionally. Men, we have our healing process, but being on the couch as a victim is NOT it. I understand that systems were built by design to put us in a position to keep us back—to keep us down. But we're stronger than that system.

1 John 4:4 tells us, "Ye are of God, little children, and have overcome them: because greater is He that is in you, than he that is in the world." Men, stand up and BE men. Being down is not who you are! I am more than a conqueror! Say

it with me! Believe it. Let Him take over your mind. "I am more than a conqueror" is a statement to get your body to obey the Father. That word "I AM" is the Name of our Father! He said, "I AM that I AM" (Exodus 3:14; 1 John 3; Hebrews 4). "Jesus Christ" means "I AM Anointed/Chosen" in Latin. My ethnicity is Creole, Hebrew, Choctaw, and French, but WHO I AM is a Son of the living God! The one who erases lack.

When I say "YAH" in Hebrew, it means "I AM."
When I say "Hallelujah:" Hallel = praises, u = to someone, and JAH, IAH or YAH = His Name, "I AM."
Hallelujah means "Praise to I AM!"
YAHuSha means I AM Salvation. Love, Joy, Peace, Meekness, Goodness, Brotherly Kindness, Temperance, Patience, Long-suffering.

"Sha" means Salvation in Hebrew.

"Ah" means Almighty. Put it together and you have YAHu SHAu AH or Yahushua, more commonly known as "Joshua," meaning "deliverance." Or in other words, again, I AM Salvation Almighty. These words were not spoken just to say "hello." Yes!!! We are to continuously sing praises to the Great I AM by BEING that very Word of God spoken in song. From the fruit of His mouth, I am because HE, my Abba Father, IS.

So now that you know, say "I am," and every time you say "I am," something you say must line up with the Word of God, or you are taking the LORD'S Name in vain. And go out, I implore you!!! No matter what you've gone through, men, rest in the Father. Go to Him for answers, go to Him for healing, go to Him for deliverance, and rise up and BE men. BE prophets, priests, and kings of your households once again.

Take some time to read Psalm 110. Decipher the code with the Ruach HaKodesh, which is The Holy Ghost. And always remember: LIFE IS A MOMENT. Infinity is in the… NOW.

EPIPHANY

# BULLET THIRTY THREE

# The Key to Understanding This Book

> This book is the testimony of what my Abba Father did to me, through me, and for me IN Him as an example of His greatness. Your actions either are or are not an example of His goodness.

### Scriptures to Study

**1 Thessalonians 4 (King James Version)**

1 Furthermore then we beseech you, brethren, and exhort you by the Lord Jesus, that as ye have received of us how ye ought to walk and to please God, so ye would abound more and more.

2 For ye know what commandments we gave you by the Lord Jesus.

3 For this is the will of God, even your sanctification, that ye should abstain from fornication:

4 That every one of you should know how to possess his vessel in sanctification and honour;

5 Not in the lust of concupiscence, even as the Gentiles which know not God:

6 That no man go beyond and defraud his brother in any matter: because that the Lord is the avenger of all such, as we also have forewarned you and testified.

7 For God hath not called us unto uncleanness, but unto holiness.

8 He therefore that despiseth, despiseth not man, but God, who hath also given unto us his holy Spirit.

9 But as touching brotherly love ye need not that I write unto you: for ye yourselves are taught of God to love one another.

10 And indeed ye do it toward all the brethren which are in all Macedonia: but we beseech you, brethren, that ye increase more and more;

11 And that ye study to be quiet, and to do your own business, and to work with your own hands, as we commanded you;

12 That ye may walk honestly toward them that are without, and that ye may have lack of nothing.

13 But I would not have you to be ignorant, brethren, concerning them which are asleep, that ye sorrow not, even as others which have no hope.

14 For if we believe that Jesus died and rose again, even so them also which sleep in Jesus will God bring with Him.

15 For this we say unto you by the word of the Lord, that we which are alive and remain unto the coming of the Lord shall not prevent them which are asleep.

16 For the Lord himself shall descend from heaven with a shout, with the voice of the archangel, and with the trump of God: and the dead in Christ shall rise first:

17 Then we which are alive and remain shall be caught up together with them in the clouds, to meet the Lord in the air: and so shall we ever be with the Lord.

18 Wherefore comfort one another with these words.

Fornication = false worship, as in "Esau fornicated against God." Look up "Zanah" in Hebrew.

LOVE is being a living sacrifice IN Him.

He is self-named as "I AM that I AM" (Exodus 3:14). The 10 Commandments were written by the finger of God Himself, and in John 14:15 He says, "If you love Me, keep My commandments." i.e., repentance from dead works of the law (Hebrews 6:1, 2)

Graduating from the Levitical priesthood, "the law," the schoolmaster (Galations 3:24) into maturity or salvation. Royal priesthood after the order of Melchizedek, resting in His face (2 Chronicles 7:14) of YAHuSHAuAH, Ha'Mishiach (I AM Salvation Almighty The Chosen, i.e., Jesus the Christ).

Read Psalm 110 and Hebrews Chapter 1. These passages are for when a person goes to sleep in the Father (the Gospel), and they are unaware of time. But we who are alive and remain are still going through the duration of time while our loved ones are asleep in the bosom of the Father, just as we are in HIM. One is the power of 0.

To my Brethren:

## Psalm 110 (King James Version)

Psalm of King David:

1 The Lord said unto my Lord, Sit thou at my right hand, until I make thine enemies thy footstool.

2 The Lord shall send the rod of thy strength out of Zion: rule thou in the midst of thine enemies.

3 Thy people shall be willing in the day of thy power, in the beauties of holiness from the womb of the morning: thou hast the dew of thy youth.

4 The Lord hath sworn, and will not repent, Thou art a priest for ever after the order of Melchizedek.

5 The Lord at thy right hand shall strike through kings in the day of His wrath.

6 He shall judge among the heathen, He shall fill the places with the dead bodies; He shall wound the heads over many countries.

7 He shall drink of the brook in the way: therefore shall He lift up the head.

Whose Son is the Christ, the Chosen, the Anointed, the Messiah, the Body? Mark 12:35-37; Luke 20:41-44

## Matthew 22:41-46 (King James Version)

41 While the Pharisees were gathered together, Jesus asked them,

42 Saying, What think ye of Christ? Whose Son is He? They say unto Him, The Son of David.

43 He saith unto them, How then doth David in spirit call him Lord, saying,

44 The LORD said unto my Lord, Sit Thou on my right hand, till I make Thine enemies thy footstool?

45 If David then call Him Lord, how is He his son?

EPIPHANY

46 And no man was able to answer Him a word, neither durst any man from that day forth ask him any more questions.

Mark 12:36 (King James Version)
For David himself said by the Holy Ghost, The Lord said to my Lord, Sit thou on my right hand, till I make Thine enemies Thy footstool.

## Acts 2:29 (The Berean Standard Bible)

29 Brothers, I can tell you with confidence that the patriarch David died and was buried, and his tomb is with us to this day.

30 But he was a prophet and knew that God had promised him on oath that He would place one of his descendants on his throne.

31 Foreseeing this, David spoke about the resurrection of the Christ, that He was not abandoned to Hades, nor did His body see decay.

32 God has raised this Jesus to life, to which we are all witnesses.

33 Exalted, then, to the right hand of God, He has received from the Father the promised Holy Spirit and has poured out what you now see and hear.

34 For David did not ascend into heaven, but he himself says:
"'The Lord said to my Lord,
"Sit at My right hand

35 until I make Your enemies a footstool for Your feet."

36 "Therefore let all Israel know with certainty that God has made this Jesus, whom you crucified, both Lord and Christ."

37 When the people heard this, they were cut to the heart and asked Peter and the other apostles, "Brothers, what shall we do?"

38 Peter replied, "Repent and be baptized, every one of you, in the name of Jesus Christ for the forgiveness of your sins, and you will receive the gift of the Holy Spirit.

39 This promise belongs to you and your children and to all who are far off—to all whom the Lord our God will call to Himself."

## Romans 9 (King James Version)

1 I say the truth in Christ, I lie not, my conscience also bearing me witness in the Holy Ghost,

2 That I have great heaviness and continual sorrow in my heart.

3 For I could wish that myself were accursed from Christ for my brethren, my kinsmen according to the flesh:

4 Who are Israelites; to whom pertaineth the adoption, and the glory, and the covenants, and the giving of the law, and the service of God, and the promises;

5 Whose are the fathers, and of whom as concerning the flesh Christ came, who is over all, God blessed for ever. Amen.

6 Not as though the word of God hath taken none effect. For they are not all Israel, which are of Israel:

7 Neither, because they are the seed of Abraham, are they all children: but, In Isaac shall thy seed be called.

8 That is, They which are the children of the flesh, these are not the children of God: but the children of the promise are counted for the seed.

9 For this is the word of promise, At this time will I come, and Sarah shall have a son.

10 And not only this; but when Rebecca also had conceived by one, even by our father Isaac;

11 (For the children being not yet born, neither having done any good or evil, that the purpose of God according to election might stand, not of works, but of him that calleth;)

12 It was said unto her, The elder shall serve the younger.

13 As it is written, Jacob have I loved, but Esau have I hated.

14 What shall we say then? Is there unrighteousness with God? God forbid.

15 For he saith to Moses, I will have mercy on whom I will have mercy, and I will have compassion on whom I will have compassion.

16 So then it is not of him that willeth, nor of him that runneth, but of God that sheweth mercy.

17 For the scripture saith unto Pharaoh, Even for this same purpose have I raised thee up, that I might shew my power in thee, and that my name might be declared throughout all the earth.

18 Therefore hath he mercy on whom he will have mercy, and whom he will he hardeneth.

19 Thou wilt say then unto me, Why doth he yet find fault? For who hath resisted his will?

20 Nay but, O man, who art thou that repliest against God? Shall the thing formed say to him that formed it, Why hast thou made me thus?

21 Hath not the potter power over the clay, of the same lump to make one vessel unto honour, and another unto dishonour?

22 What if God, willing to shew his wrath, and to make his power known, endured with much longsuffering the vessels of wrath fitted to destruction:

23 And that he might make known the riches of his glory on the vessels of mercy, which he had afore prepared unto glory,

24 Even us, whom he hath called, not of the Jews only, but also of the Gentiles?

25 As he saith also in Osee, I will call them my people, which were not my people; and her beloved, which was not beloved.

26 And it shall come to pass, that in the place where it was said unto them, Ye are not my people; there shall they be called the children of the living God.

27 Esaias also crieth concerning Israel, Though the number of the children of Israel be as the sand of the sea, a remnant shall be saved:

28 For he will finish the work, and cut it short in righteousness: because a short work will the Lord make upon the earth.

29 And as Esaias said before, Except the Lord of Sabaoth had left us a seed, we had been as Sodoma, and been made like unto Gomorrha.

30 What shall we say then? That the Gentiles, which followed not after righteousness, have attained to righteousness, even the righteousness which is of faith.

31 But Israel, which followed after the law of righteousness, hath not attained to the law of righteousness.

32 Wherefore? Because they sought it not by faith, but as it were by the works of the law. For they stumbled at that stumblingstone;

33 As it is written, Behold, I lay in Sion a stumblingstone and rock of offence: and whosoever believeth on him shall not be ashamed.

## Isaiah 11 (King James Version)

1 And there shall come forth a rod out of the stem of Jesse, and a Branch shall grow out of his roots:

2 And the spirit of the Lord shall rest upon him, the spirit of wisdom and understanding, the spirit of counsel and might, the spirit of knowledge and of the fear of the Lord;

3 And shall make him of quick understanding in the fear of the Lord: and he shall not judge after the sight of his eyes, neither reprove after the hearing of his ears:

4 But with righteousness shall he judge the poor, and reprove with equity for the meek of the earth: and he shall smite the earth: with the rod of his mouth, and with the breath of his lips shall he slay the wicked.

5 And righteousness shall be the girdle of his loins, and faithfulness the girdle of his reins.

6 The wolf also shall dwell with the lamb, and the leopard shall lie down with the kid; and the calf and the young lion and the fatling together; and a little child shall lead them.

7 And the cow and the bear shall feed; their young ones shall lie down together: and the lion shall eat straw like the ox.

8 And the sucking child shall play on the hole of the asp, and the weaned child shall put his hand on the cockatrice' den.

9 They shall not hurt nor destroy in all my holy mountain: for the earth shall be full of the knowledge of the Lord, as the waters cover the sea.

10 And in that day there shall be a root of Jesse, which shall stand for an ensign of the people; to it shall the Gentiles seek: and his rest shall be glorious.

11 And it shall come to pass in that day, that the Lord shall set his hand again the second time to recover the remnant of his people, which shall be left, from Assyria, and from Egypt, and from Pathros, and from Cush, and from Elam, and from Shinar, and from Hamath, and from the islands of the sea.

12 And he shall set up an ensign for the nations, and shall assemble the outcasts of Israel, and gather together the dispersed of Judah from the four corners of the earth.

13 The envy also of Ephraim shall depart, and the adversaries of Judah shall be cut off: Ephraim shall not envy Judah, and Judah shall not vex Ephraim.

14 But they shall fly upon the shoulders of the Philistines toward the west; they shall spoil them of the east together: they shall lay their hand upon Edom and Moab; and the children of Ammon shall obey them.

15 And the Lord shall utterly destroy the tongue of the Egyptian sea; and with his mighty wind shall he shake his hand over the river, and shall smite it in the seven streams, and make men go over dryshod.

16 And there shall be an highway for the remnant of his people, which shall be left, from Assyria; like as it was to Israel in the day that he came up out of the land of Egypt.

## Isaiah 61 (King James Version)

The Year of the Lord's Favor

(Matthew 2:19-23; Matthew 13:53-58; Mark 6:1-6; Luke 2:39-40; Luke 4:16-30)

1 The Spirit of the Lord GOD is upon me; because the LORD hath anointed me to preach good tidings unto the meek; he hath sent me to bind up the brokenhearted, to proclaim liberty to the captives, and the opening of the prison to them that are bound;

2 To proclaim the acceptable year of the LORD, and the day of vengeance of our God; to comfort all that mourn;

3 To appoint unto them that mourn in Zion, to give unto them beauty for ashes, the oil of joy for mourning, the garment of praise for the spirit of heaviness; that they might be called trees of righteousness, the planting of the LORD, that he might be glorified.

4 And they shall build the old wastes, they shall raise up the former desolations, and they shall repair the waste cities, the desolations of many generations.

5 And strangers shall stand and feed your flocks, and the sons of the alien shall be your plowmen and your vinedressers.

6 But ye shall be named the Priests of the LORD: men shall call you the Ministers of our God: ye shall eat the riches of the Gentiles, and in their glory shall ye boast yourselves.

7 For your shame ye shall have double; and for confusion they shall rejoice in their portion: therefore in their land they shall possess the double: everlasting joy shall be unto them.

8 For I the LORD love judgment, I hate robbery for burnt offering; and I will direct their work in truth, and I will make an everlasting covenant with them.

9 And their seed shall be known among the Gentiles, and their offspring among the people: all that see them shall acknowledge them, that they are the seed which the LORD hath blessed.

# EPIPHANY

10 I will greatly rejoice in the LORD, my soul shall be joyful in my God; for he hath clothed me with the garments of salvation, he hath covered me with the robe of righteousness, as a bridegroom decketh himself with ornaments, and as a bride adorneth herself with her jewels.

11 For as the earth bringeth forth her bud, and as the garden causeth the things that are sown in it to spring forth; so the Lord GOD will cause righteousness and praise to spring forth before all the nations.

Just comforting those who mourn...Grand Rising, beauty for ashes (Isaiah 61:3) 🕊️ 🔥

> I am 6 years old. Elder Ross asks me if I know what $E = mc^2$ is? It's to become the Word... Keep coming (Matthew 14:28, 29)

**Special thanks to Mom. There are no words...**

# Songs of Marshon KenYatta Goode Peoples

## "I AM Embraced" written by MarShon Goode-Peoples

**(Chorus)**
I AM... His love, His grace
I AM... Sin Erased
I AM... Patience, His Face
I AM... Father Son embraced.

**(Verse 1)**
I AM... a bomb in Gilead! Havoc wreakin!
I have what I say so... I got to speakin.
I AM a Son... of the Great I AM
How do you know? Cause I said I AM.
Watch my actions,
match His coming attractions
by rightly dividing ABBAs Word...
BOOM! ...subtract man's fear fractions.
Minds lit up like a HOLY "new clear" reaction.

**(Verse 2)**
Did you read down to the sticks? Don't be scared.
Transformation happens... Like your crucifix. But devil's beware.
Transformers came from the Kidron
Golgotha decision making,
knowledge, understanding and wisdom, in HIM, hidden treasures there.

## "The Heavens Declare" written by MarShon Goode-Peoples

Unto the end from the beginning
ALL praises go to my God with worship and with singing
Bringing me closer to The Father
I hear the question you asked in your mind, "Why bother?"

Because He's is as like a bridegroom that cometh out of His Chamber
To see what He's purchased with His blood; the Church, His bride, I AM a part…
That's why to him I AM, NO stranger!

Before the foundation of the world He knew me…
With the Foreknowledge of His Word He grew me.
He came to Earth through Virgin birth to be crucified for the world.

So I no longer wonder why He chooses me.
That's why from day to day I utter His speech as I preach and I teach…
And night to night I show forth His Power by RESTing in HIM as I sleep.

There is no speech nor language that the Heavenly has not heard…
of the Firmermanent, showing forth His magnificent, wonderful and awesome handiwork!

*(Continued)*

I AM part of the same as I proclaim Jesus YAHuSHAuAH Ha'Mishiach's NAME...
To make you aware, devil's beware, of the Glory of My God... That the heavens declare.

### "I AM Alright" written by MarShon Goode-Peoples

I'm here to say my testimony…
I'm proof that God would never leave.

A Designated Bullet called Epiphany…
Struck me in my head, I'm dead, but God told me to, "Breathe…"

I'm alright.
Timelessness in His presence
Until now, I thought I knew peace.

I feel like I AM floating
What's happening to me?
"Don't worry My child." He said that HE had to carry me

Now, I AM alright.

## "Resuscitate" written by MarShon Goode-Peoples

I've sat with powerful pastors in my past
Now I sit and sup with The Powerful Apostle... He IS a Blast!
He's like 3 "New Clear" effective explosions!
Not idling sitting spiritually eroding...

Coroden...like Eli, that crip keeper, letting God's lamp go dim, for religious sleepers. I PEEP cha!
Then I moved on...
The Son came up, yeah I woke up, now I'm gone.

On a sabbatical, to be fanatical.
Molded, taught and encouraged to be radical.
Then deployed...for hellish systems to be destroyed.
What?! Devils y'all annoyed?

Cuz I'm all loaded and cocked up!
With the Word of God's Spirit filled Faith rocked up!
A lethal weapon, unlike Mel Gibson, I got the "True Passion of Christ" PEACE!

So don't get it twisted. Leaders of that old school made that same mistake. Paradox! I'm like a earthquake.
I shake rocks, like The Nation and Livestock dissertations
Better yet, I stand on The ROCK and wreck demonic foundations.

EPIPHANY

## "Introduction" written by MarShon Goode-Peoples

I am the 'm' to the 'a' to the r s h o n... listen to my rhyme as my saga begins
I'm a christener minista all demons I will diminish ya with the word of God I'll cut you up and finish ya.

I'm too blessed, to be stressed, to worry about your mess
I'm one of the ones, wait that equals seven... with righteousness written across his chest I profess.

Holiness no holy facade but child of God "show stopper"
I even got a holy cool walk like Bishop Harper
Don't let me time you Devils cuz I will clock ya then use the shield of faith that God gave me just to block ya

To please my Lord to delight him to show favor, that's why our love is sweeter than a honeycomb flavor
Taste and see that my Lord is good and become a holy warrior of His royal priesthood

A part of his flock like Enoch translated, like him I'm heaven bound by the Blood now my life is unfated.

## "Light of Eternal Mind" written by MarShon Goode-Peoples

For I see through the clouds of despair cuz I know that you are there

Waiting for me with arms wide
Because of You Lord I know I can hide

From the cataclysmic treachery that comes against me, and in you Lord I know I am free

Where I found that Your love is so kind, You're my light of eternal mind.

I was down in the misty valley of discouragement when your two edged Word cut through all my doubts.

You made me a Son of your Wholeness. In fact which I cannot BE without.

Now I stand in Your awesome and mighty bulwark where slavery of sin is not my plight. I'm a warrior of Your holy arsenal a part of an infantry of Your children ready to fight.

You're my light of eternal mind (x3 overlap). Light of eternal mind!

Light of eternal mind, You're my light of eternal mind. Light of eternal mind, You're my light of eternal mind.

EPIPHANY

## "Queen (Come Here)..." written by MarShon Goode-Peoples

Mi K'mere ici amore, Je'suis Goode-Peuple' MarChon. Pardon major excut le pur Francois Mademoiselle. May I tell?

This "Breastplate" is made for peace so just rest ,your Head on this chest of ABBA Father's WHOLENESS.

ABBA's Word hides there YeruSalem My heart resides there I AM where He abide. Ui lil ici si "Here" you SEE me

# About the Author

## A Triumph of Resilience and a Beacon of Inspiration

In the tapestry of human stories, MarShon Peoples stands as a living testament to the indomitable strength of the human spirit. He is not just a survivor but a force of motivation, a living testament to the extraordinary power of resilience, and a catalyst for change. MarShon's journey, from sustaining a life-altering gunshot wound to the head to authoring the impactful book *Epiphany: The Designated Bullet*, is a story of determination, healing, and an unwavering commitment to empowering others.

## A Defining Moment

MarShon's life underwent a radical transformation at a critical juncture that he could have allowed to define him. Instead, he defied the odds, using adversity as an opportunity for unparalleled growth. Emerging from the challenges of recovery and self-discovery, MarShon, with God as his strength, transcended the role of a mere survivor, evolving into a passionate advocate for the transformative power of faith and resilience.

### The Healing Pen

MarShon found healing through the strokes of his pen. With his words, he extends that healing touch to others. As an author, his book *Epiphany: The Designated Bullet* not only narrates his personal triumph but also serves as a beacon of hope for those navigating their own challenges.

### Motivational Dynamo

As a motivational speaker, MarShon is a dynamic force, captivating audiences with his unique perspective on life. He doesn't just tell his story; he invites others to be part of the narrative, encouraging them to tap into their inner strength, triumph over adversity, and strive for greatness.

### Empowering Narratives

MarShon's speaking engagements cover a spectrum of empowering topics, including Overcoming Adversity, Finding Purpose and Meaning, Building Resilience and Mental Strength, Embracing Change, and Empowering Others

## Mentorship to Young Minds

Beyond the stage, MarShon is a mentor to boys and young men, imparting wisdom and guidance as they navigate the complexities of adolescence. His commitment to nurturing the next generation reflects a profound dedication to creating a legacy of resilience and empowerment.

In MarShon Peoples, we find not just a survivor but a luminary, illuminating the path toward triumph over adversity. His story is not just one of overcoming; it's a celebration of the human spirit's boundless capacity for growth and healing through reliance on the Almighty God.

For More Information About

The Author Visit

WWW.GOODEPEOPLES.COM

# MARSHON PEOPLES

www.ingramcontent.com/pod-product-compliance
Lightning Source LLC
LaVergne TN
LVHW041658060526
838201LV00043B/478